Managing Language Diversity

KW-278-597

CURRENT ISSUES IN LANGUAGE AND SOCIETY

Editorial Board
Dennis Ager, Paul Chilton, Helen Kelly-Holmes, Christina Schäffner and Sue Wright are all members of the Institute for the Study of Language and Society at Aston University, Birmingham

Other Books in the Series
Analysing Political Speeches
  CHRISTINA SCHÄFFNER (ed.)
Children Talking: The Development of Pragmatic Competence
  LINDA THOMPSON (ed.)
Cultural Functions of Translation
  CHRISTINA SCHÄFFNER and HELEN KELLY-HOLMES (eds)
Discourse and Ideologies
  CHRISTINA SCHÄFFNER and HELEN KELLY-HOLMES (eds)
Ethnicity in Eastern Europe: Questions of Migration, Language Rights and Education
  SUE WRIGHT (ed.)
Language and the State: Revitalization and Revival in Israel and Eire
  SUE WRIGHT (ed.)
Languages in Contact and Conflict: Contrasting Experiences in the Netherlands and Belgium
  SUE WRIGHT (ed.)
Managing Language Diversity
  SUE WRIGHT and HELEN-KELLY HOLMES (eds)
Monolingualism and Bilingualism: Lessons from Canada and Spain
  SUE WRIGHT (ed.)
One Country, Two Systems, Three Languages: A Survey of Changing Language Use in Hong Kong
  SUE WRIGHT and HELEN KELLY-HOLMES (eds)
Translation and Quality
  CHRISTINA SCHÄFFNER (ed.)

Please contact us for the latest book information:
Multilingual Matters Ltd, Frankfurt Lodge, Clevedon Hall,
Victoria Road, Clevedon, BS21 7HH, England

UNIVERSITY COLLEGE CHICHESTER LIBRARIES

AUTHOR:	WS 2163585 4
TITLE: MANAGING	CLASS No: 404.2
DATE: July 2000	SUBJECT: CIEM

Managing Language Diversity

Edited by
Sue Wright and Helen Kelly-Holmes

MULTILINGUAL MATTERS LTD
Clevedon • Philadelphia • Toronto • Sydney • Johannesburg

Library of Congress Cataloging in Publication Data

Managing Language Diversity/Edited by Sue Wright and Helen Kelly-Holmes
Includes bibliographical references
1. Multilingualism–Australia. 2. Multiculturalism–Australia. 3. Language policy–Australia.
4. Language and education–Australia. I. Wright, Sue. II. Kelly-Holmes, Helen. III. Clyne,
Michael G. IV. Current Issues in Language and Society.
P115.5.A8M36   1998
309.44'994–dc21   97-47652

British Library Cataloguing in Publication Data

A CIP catalogue record for this book is available from the British Library.

ISBN 1-85359-415-6 (hbk)

Multilingual Matters Ltd

UK: Frankfurt Lodge, Clevedon Hall, Victoria Road, Clevedon BS21 7HH.
USA: 1900 Frost Road, Suite 101, Bristol, PA 19007, USA.
Canada: OISE, 712 Gordon Baker Road, Toronto, Ontario, Canada M2H 3R7.
Australia: P.O. Box 586, Artamon, NSW, Australia.
South Africa: PO Box 1080, Northcliffe 2115, Johannesburg, South Africa.

Copyright © 1998 Sue Wright, Helen Kelly-Holmes and the authors of individual articles.

This book is also available as Vol. 4, No. 2 of the journal *Current Issues in Language and Society*.

All rights reserved. No part of this work may be reproduced in any form or by any means
without permission in writing from the publisher.

Printed and bound in Great Britain by Short Run Press.

Contents

Reconciling Inclusion, Multiculturalism and Multilingualism

Sue Wright
Institute for the Study of Language and Society, Aston University, Aston Triangle, Birmingham B4 7ET, UK.

Two sets of tensions coexist in most situations of migration prompted by economic considerations. The first tension derives from the conflicting aims of the economic migrants themselves. They need to adapt to the new situation in which they find themselves in order to make the most of the new economic possibilities for which they have come. At the same time, they are unlikely to wish to relinquish their religious, social, cultural and linguistic heritage, assuming that most migration which takes place for economic reasons does not necessarily imply a rejection of the country of origin.

The second tension derives from the conflicting aims of the host society. For any receiving group which treats incomers as citizens and allows and expects them to play a full role in democratic and civic society, there is the need to incorporate the new group, according them the same rights, duties and opportunities as members of the host community. Without such incorporation the solidarity and community necessary for a democracy are deemed not to be possible (Mill, 1948). But full assimilation would mean the domination of the incomers by the host society and a failure on the latter's part to value the contribution of the new members. Refusing to make space for different ways of doing things would fail to capitalise on diversity and would lead to feelings of resentment on the part of the incomers towards those demanding such sacrifices.

For a society to manage these conflicting aims needs immense generosity of spirit. On the part of the host society, the generosity comes through offering the possibility of full integration but accepting that certain aspects of integration may be declined, and that this is the right of the immigrants. For the incoming group, the generosity comes from its willingness to accept the adjustments that the hosts demand, or at least enough of them for the host society to believe that they are maintaining the cohesive solidarity of their society.

For the individual to manage these conflicting aims needs immense skill. Fitting oneself and one's family to be socially mobile and economically successful in a new context may demand assuming some of the cultural values of the host society. Since such social mobility and economic success are the prime reasons for economic migration, immigrants are likely to feel that geographical upheaval would be pointless without the concomitant cultural, linguistic and social effort necessary to benefit fully from the venture. At the same time, few would wish to divest themselves of the religious, linguistic and cultural influences which have formed them. To do so would be to enter a rootless world and to court anomie. The skill is in incorporating both old and new allegiances into a new *hyphenated* identity and in convincing the members of each non-hyphenated group that one's membership of that group is valid and committed.

Nowhere are these individual and societal tensions more salient than in the question of language. Language is, along with religion, the clearest, most rooted and least negotiable marker of identity. For a group, it has a symbolic function and is the practical means by which the group associates, remembers its history and plans its future. For an individual, it is a badge of identity and a requirement for membership of the community of communication.

In the situation of migration language is usually problematic. The host community that wishes to extend full membership to the newcomers will require the language skills necessary for that to be possible, and this is particularly true of the democratic society where political life is a discursive activity. However, the minority constituted by immigration will also wish to conserve the language of the country of origin. It preserves their specificity and allows them to congregate as a discrete group, something which may be more or less valued according to whether the group's religion requires endogamy, distinctive practices and a particular moral code.

For the individual, acquiring a fluent command of the language of the host society is one step towards the social mobility and economic success planned as an outcome of migration. The employment which will ensure economic success is the employment which is language dependent, and so the requirement for language skills remains true whether the immigrant wishes merely to acquire capital before returning to the country of origin or to settle permanently in the new country. But at the same time the language of the country of origin is the channel by which contact with family, friends and business networks will be maintained and through which access can be had to the individual's cultural heritage. The solution to these tensions would thus seem to be individual bilingualism within societal diglossia for that part of the nation constituted by recent immigration.

The papers in this issue of the journal reflect on the problems, compromises and strategies inherent in achieving personal bilingualism and maintaining the languages of immigrant groups. The context here is Australia. Michael Clyne reveals the realities of the situation, recording which groups are retaining their languages and suggesting why this is so. He then analyses past and present government policy at both national and regional level and shows the effect this has had on individual and group language maintenance. He reports on two studies recently completed by his institute and ends with a heart-felt plea for diversity, tolerance of diversity and a recognition that the state ought to help bear the costs of what may constitute the common good. The comments and questions which follow were part of the debate which took place at the CILS seminar where Michael presented his paper. The responses have all been written by scholars who attended that meeting. John Joseph argues that there is no essential link between language and culture and deplores the sometimes spurious ways that language professionals have sought to exploit the link. He coins the term a *splendid* multiculturalism and hopes that it will be available to all pupils and students, from all sectors of society, both host and constituted by recent immigration. Dennis Smith directs attention to the power relationships that mould a nation's language policy and provides a working definition of cultural democracy. Stephen May evaluates how firmly rooted multiculturalism and multilingualism might be in Australia. Li Wei provides us with a paradigm for investigating the issue of language maintenance. Vanithanami Saravanan cites Singapore as an example of the positive cultural effects deriving from a market driven language-in-education policy. Jane Stuart-Smith bears witness to the experience of the *non-background* learner in the mixed language class and provides an insight into the possible disadvantages experienced by the learner with *background*. Dennis Ager discusses the issue of possible backlash in the host community against perceived 'unfairness'. Finally, Helen Kelly-Holmes rounds off this issue with a personal piece based on her own early experience in a language maintenance classroom.

The complexity of the reactions to Michael Clyne are an indication of the impossibility of finding any single, glib solution to the problem of maintaining language and culture within migrant groups. We are agreed that the goal of inclusion is a worthy one, but not easily managed alongside policies to safeguard cultural diversity and plurilingualism. We are agreed that economic imperatives often militate against diversity, both at the level of individual choices and government policy. The challenge is to reconcile unity and diversity, and to do so in ways which we can afford. If we could achieve this, then such a model would be useful for all societies torn between the magnet of globalisation and the desire to preserve their specificity.

References

Mill J.S. (1861, this edn 1948) *Considerations on Representative Government.* Oxford: Blackwell.

Managing Language Diversity and Second Language Programmes in Australia

Michael Clyne
Department of Linguistics/Language and Society Centre, Language Australia,
Monash University, Menzies Building, Wellington Road, Clayton 3168, Victoria,
Australia

This paper discusses the position of community languages in Australia against a background of changing anti-social policies across all areas, in the direction of economic rationalism and user pays. The paper also explores languages-in-education policies in relation to school second language programmes which need to cater for students with no background and different degrees of learning in the language. Some suggestions are made for managing linguistic diversity. There is a discussion of what happens when a community language also becomes a coveted commodity for the whole of the population. The historical context for the development of pluralistic policies in the 1970s and 1980s and for more recent challenges to them, especially from the political fringe, are discussed. It is hoped that these considerations of the Australian situation may be of wider application.

Introduction

> The thing that distresses me most is how little children and grandchildren of overseas-born Australians retain of the culture and especially the language of their lands of origin. The loss of ancestral language is grievous for the individual and the nation. We should be a nation of great linguists.

> *(The Age*, 27 January 1989)

This statement came not from a committed linguist but from none other than Sir Ninian Stephen in his final Australia Day address to the nation as Governor-General on 26 January, 1989.

It expresses a widespread attitude in Australia and a proven reality. It is widely accepted that Australia's language resources are of value to the nation as well as to the individual, in the interests of social justice and cohesion, cultural enrichment, and economic assets. Yet these resources are still being wasted. This paper uses the current Australian situation to highlight two broad issues:

(1) What happens when the same language is both a language of wider teaching and a community language?

(2) What happens to a socially motivated language policy intended to further cultural democracy (Smolicz *et al.*, 1984) when rampant economic rationalism sets in and takes over education and all other public domains?

The paper examines the language shift statistics across a number of community languages and draws on recent small-scale studies relating language maintenance and school language study. In the context of the disintegration of comprehensive and co-ordinated national languages policy, economic rationalisation and anti-social attitudes, it examines the way in which state languages-in-education policies and practice attempt to address both language needs and the dilemma of catering in second language programmes for students with no background and different degrees of background in the language. It argues for a strategy for not only maintaining but also developing our language resources. It addresses such issues as the continuum of backgrounds in a language, the activation of passive skills, and reactivation of lost skills. The need for continuing policy formulation and implementation is discussed. This includes models and curricula for multi-level classes. It is suggested that the further development of English-plus requires co-operation between communities and school systems. Due to the exigencies of globalisation and European integration, this issue is likely to be of increasing relevance to other countries too.

Language Maintenance and Shift

The 1991 Census, the most recent for which there is language-use data currently available, indicated that 14.8% of the Australian population used a language other than English in the home. This proportion is much higher in Melbourne (26%) and Sydney (24.9%), which have attracted the majority of the immigrants, and the Northern Territory, where most of the Aboriginal languages are used (25.3%). It should be noted that recent censuses have requested information only on language use in one's own home. Regular use in other domains and venues, including one's parents' home would increase the above percentage considerably. Table 1 shows the most widely used community languages in Australia. I would boldly predict that, in the August 1996 Census, Spanish will enter the 100,000 group, Greek will be surpassed by the aggregated Chinese numbers, and Vietnamese will replace German as community language No. 5.

Table 1 Most widely used community languages in Australia across states

	1991 Figures								
	NSW	*VIC*	*Q'LD*	*SA*	*WA*	*TAS*	*NT*	*ACT*	*AUST*
Arabic	117,826	34,802	2,890	3,194	2,740	322	120	963	162,857
Chinese	118,780	75,672	21,309	9,594	23,035	1,270	2,007	4,534	256,201
'Yugoslav' Serbian Serbo-Croatian Croatian	51,078	46,732	7,656	8,563	11,222	583	178	4,727	130,739
German	34,290	32,441	16,846	14,872	9,149	2,125	918	2,695	113,336
Greek	98,522	132,489	11,360	29,904	6,291	1,452	2,567	3,142	285,700
Italian	113,818	179,324	26,947	48,810	42,995	1,788	960	4,162	418,804
Spanish	48,277	23,575	7,253	3,134	4,864	456	350	2,570	90,947
Vietnamese	42,472	9,459	8,758	9,022	7,915	228	447	1,886	110,187

The two major cities, Sydney and Melbourne, have drifted apart in their ethnolinguistic profiles. Melbourne, building on the mainly European immigration of the post-war period, has strong concentrations of languages such as Greek, Macedonian, Maltese, Turkish and Italian. Sydney has attracted strong concentrations of some of the 'newer' community languages from beyond Europe, e.g. Arabic, (Latin American) Spanish, Chinese, Filipino, Korean, and Hindi. In fact, while Italian and Greek are still the most widely used community languages in Melbourne, they have been replaced in Sydney by Chinese and Arabic. (In the school age population in Sydney, Italian is now in fifth position.)

Because of the younger age profiles of the Arabic- and Chinese-speaking communities, this change will also affect Melbourne soon, as can be predicted from Table 2.

Table 2 Language use at home, 0–14 age group

Language	Sydney	Melbourne
Arabic	38,663	11,316
Chinese (aggregated)	21,546	13,349
Greek	13,956	18,873
Italian	10,723	18,513
Vietnamese	10,864	10,834

In terms of maintenance of community languages in the home, there is differential behaviour in the various ethnolinguistic groups. Table 3 shows that the same rank order of language maintenance/shift applies to the first and second generations, and regardless of whether they are products of an exogamous or endogamous marriage. However, generation and family marriage pattern play crucial roles in the extent of language shift. The statistics show that, of the older established ethnic groups, 57% of those born in the Netherlands indicated that they speak only English in the home, whereas this was the case only for 4.4% of those born in Greece. Those born in Germany, and Malta, as well as Austria (42.5%), France (31.5%), Hungary (26.7%), and Spain (16.5%) fall somewhere between the Dutch end and the middle of the continuum. Those born in Latin-America (6.3%) and Turkey (3.8%), together with more recent Asian groups (see below), are among the most retentive ethnolinguistic communities. The possible reasons have been discussed elsewhere (e.g. Clyne, 1991, Clyne & Kipp, 1996, Pauwels, 1995, Smolicz *et al.*, 1989/90) and we do not need to go in to them here. Relative population size, age, gender, the role of language in the group's or individual's cultural value system (and its intertwining with other core values), cultural distance/ similarity, networks, and knowledge of English all play a role, and they tend to work together. What is really stunning is the high language shift over time in the second generation. It is the fourth column that is really significant since that takes into account the exogamy rate of the specific language community.

These are the only groups for whom we have the full range of statistics. We have not included Egypt-, Vietnam- and Yugoslav-born because of the diversity of first languages. We are continuing to make representations to the Bureau of

Table 3 Use of English only in the home, first generation and second generation (from endogamous marriages, exogamous marriages and both aggregated)

Birthplace of self or parent(s)	1st	2nd (endo)	2nd (exo)	2nd (aggreg)
Netherlands	57.0	88.7	97.5	95.0
Germany	42.4	72.9	92.0	88.7
Malta	31.0	63.5	93.2	78.5
Poland	17.2	56.6	85.9	74.4
Italy	11.2	32.2	77.0	49.8
Hong Kong	8.4	9.6	52.5	40.0
China	5.9	21.6	58.9	45.5
Greece	4.4	9.6	53.8	21.8

Source: Taken from Clyne and Kipp (1996: 5, 8, 9), based on 1991 Census.

Statistics for a first language question to complement the home use one in the 2001 Census.

It is not only the less retentive communities where the language seems to have a predominantly two-generation life cycle. Italian experiences a 445% inter-generational rise in shift, and there is anecdotal information from depth studies that indicates that the second generation use of Italian (in contrast to that of many others) is probably overstated because it often covers an Italian ethnolect of Australian English where a limited number of Italian items are embedded into English as the matrix language, in Myers-Scotton's terms. The group that has stood out consistently as resisting language shift has been Greek-Australians. These statistics show that even they are not immune to it as the second generation provides the basis for the third generation's bilingual development, especially when exogamy increases. The higher language shift for the Hong Kong migrants than for those born in the PRC may be attributed to the presence of English and strong British cultural influence in Hong Kong and the lower status and market place value of Cantonese, in comparison with Mandarin, used by the majority of migrants from the PRC. The high inter-generational language maintenance for the Hong Kong group may then seem somewhat surprising. The reason for this may be seen in the continuing close business and family links with the homeland which result in frequent visits to the original place of origin, in comparison with the PRC descended group. Another factor is business networks in Australia (cf. Li Wei, 1994). The first generation shift for Taiwan migrants is 3%; second generation statistics are unavailable for this group as there are very few in this category.

Earlier School Assessment Policy

The story of language shift is one that has repeated itself many times throughout Australia's history. We need to consider that the parents came into an Australia committed to instantaneous assimilation. This is reflected in the education system. In the 1960s, a very narrow range of languages was taught in schools — mainly French and Latin, and in some schools in some states, German.

However, several other languages were available for examination. Students could take classes on Saturday mornings or learn them privately or prepare themselves for the examination. The presence of students speaking a community language was usually seen as a deterrent rather than an incentive to the teaching of that language at school. Some states maintained discriminatory examination assessment procedures for languages such as German, Italian and Russian.

Those who did not have full native competence in English were penalised because of their English in translations even though they were already disadvantaged by having to take all their other examinations in English. Marking systems in LOTEs (Languages other than English) were devised to penalise second generation bilinguals, and different assessment procedures were used for students identified, on the basis of an anonymous oral examination, as having a family background in the language. Some schools gave their students instruction on how not to be spotted as having a background. Many students dropped the language in which they had a background and continued with French, in which they would not suffer discrimination. They couldn't be bothered with language maintenance, which appeared to be a liability. In Victoria, this practice came to an end in 1966 when the Chair of the Schools Board's standardisation committee described it as 'distasteful'. The new procedure adopted was for some languages to be given a disproportionate number of high grades to encourage students of all backgrounds.

Impact of Multiculturalism Policy

By 1973 the policy of multiculturalism was introduced, at a time of change. (The term itself, which has many interpretations, in the Australian context stands for the recognition of cultural diversity and of multiple identity.) There were a number of strong motivations for this policy. It was part of a social reform programme of the Whitlam government, following many years of Conservative administration. Multiculturalism therefore played a role in recreating Australia as a more just society. It was part of a world-wide paradigm shift to an acceptance of difference. It also constituted an important response to a need for a new national identity in a vacuum created by the loosening of ties with Britain following the British retreat from east of Suez and its entry into the European Community. Australia's cultural diversity gave it a basis to redefine itself as an independent nation of the Asia-Pacific region.

In 1972, the White Australia Policy was finally dismantled. Lobbies in favour of multiculturalism succeeded in gaining status for community languages. Public announcements were made in a range of languages according to need. A telephone interpreter service was established, which is now operating in about 90 languages, and which during the Australian night is now providing services for the multicultural population of Britain! Government- and government-subsidised radio stations transmit programmes in over 60 languages while a government-run multicultural TV channel shows films and news broadcasts, in a variety of languages, the former all with English subtitles. Local public libraries have holdings of adults' and children's books, periodicals and cassettes in the principal community languages of the district. By 1973, too, the restrictions on the introduction of additional languages as subjects for the Year 12 examination (end of secondary school and university entrance) were lifted, first in Victoria and then in other states. There are now 38 languages examined, including Czech, Farsi, Hungarian, Khmer, Latvian, Macedonian, Maltese, Turkish, Vietnamese, Australian Sign Language (AUSLAN), and Australian Indigenous Languages. This last subject includes an in-depth study of a still spoken or revived language and a linguistic overview of Aboriginal languages and Torres Strait Island languages (AILF, 1993). Five additional languages are about to be accredited. Three of the state education departments have a section responsible for teaching languages chosen by students that are not offered at their own school. This tuition is provided on Saturdays at state high schools that function as centres for this purpose. In Victoria, 20 centres teach 40 languages between them. This is in addition to any senior secondary classes of part-time ethnic schools which teach one language across age groups. At the same time, the range of languages taught in day schools has been greatly increased since the late 1960s and they are taught in primary as well as secondary schools. There has been a mainstreaming of language maintenance, replacing the earlier state of affairs where ethnic groups were required to bear financial responsibility for Saturday schools, the community language media, and library resources. These developments all preceded the development of explicit language policy.

Explicit Language Policy

The process of evolution of a national languages policy was participatory, commencing as it did with a public inquiry conducted by parliamentarians from both the Government and the Opposition, with 12 months of hearings with evidence from 94 witnesses and 241 submissions from individuals and organisations. This set the guiding principles for future language policy:

(1) Competence in English.
(2) Maintenance and development of languages other than English (both Aboriginal and community languages).
(3) Provision of services in languages other than English.
(4) Opportunities for second language learning. (Senate, 1984)

These principles formed the basis of the *National Policy on Languages* (Lo Bianco, 1987), which stressed the complementarity of English and Australia's other languages, and the principles were absorbed into future language policies at both federal and state levels. Drawing on local and international research, the NPL was based on a sophisticated rationale, encompassing social justice, long-term economic strategies, and cultural enrichment for all Australians. Because responsibility for the National Policy on Languages was allocated to the Minister for Education, the emphasis was on education, and issues relating to media, interpreting, and public services were included only marginally, detracting from the comprehensive scope of the intended policy. The balanced approach of language policy in NPL gave way to a stress on short-term economic goals, especially the achievement of labour market needs when this started to dominate all decision-making in education and the Education portfolio was merged with Employment and Training. This new line was reflected in *Australia's Language: The Australian Language and Literacy Policy* (Dawkins, 1991), which was a top-down document though the public had been able to comment on a preceding green paper which had aroused widespread condemnation for its monocentric direction, starting from the title, *The Language of Australia*, hardly appropriate in a multilingual country. The guiding principles of the Senate Report were reiterated in the second, companion volume but there was a strong emphasis on user pays in the ESL component and an instrumental emphasis on English literacy. Aboriginal language maintenance programmes were marginalised and LOTEs were promoted through a financial prioritisation system. Schools or school systems were to receive $300 per capita for students successfully completing the Year 12 examination in a priority language. For this purpose, 14 languages were earmarked nationally:

> Arabic, Australian Aboriginal languages (taken as a group), Chinese, French, German, Indonesian, Italian, Japanese, Korean, Modern Greek, Russian, Spanish, Thai and Vietnamese,

and each state and territory required to prioritise eight of these. You are reminded that Australia has six states and two territories each with a separate education system. Moreover, about a third of schoolchildren (more in Victoria) attend non-government schools. Each state now has its own languages-in-education policy and there is considerable variation between them in entry age into language programmes and choice of languages due to geographical, economic and demographic considerations, and of course, each school, family and individual have their various reasons for choosing one language over another.

State Prioritisation

All states have a commitment for all students to take a LOTE in the compulsory years of secondary education and most are facilitating the more widespread introduction of LOTEs into primary schools. There are sometimes highly ambitious time-tables, such as the full implementation of the policy by the end of the decade despite a serious shortage of language teachers, especially in primary schools. The state implementation of these Commonwealth initiatives has led to large increases in student numbers in junior secondary language programmes. In order to maximise financial benefits, some states prioritised those languages currently with the highest enrolments. This has resulted, for instance, in the inclusion of Modern Greek in six out of eight states and territories and of Vietnamese in four, to the exclusion of Spanish (prioritised in only three). Since ALLP, national language policy has vanished from the arena of public participation and disintegrated into a number of single-issue policies such as Rudd (1994) on Asian languages and Lo Bianco (1997) on literacy. The Rudd Report presents a strategy for the promotion of Asian languages in schools — Indonesian, Japanese, Korean and Mandarin, but not Vietnamese. In effect, it provided a new reprioritisation which relegated all the other languages to an inferior position (60% to study the four 'Asian priority languages' by 2006 and 40% the other ten, with $26m over three years going to support the former four languages and $4m per year to support the other ten. No state has actually prioritised Korean).

This was in accordance with the policy of Asianisation in the interests of becoming part of a regional trade bloc. It should be noted that with the emphasis on business migration, i.e. the category of immigrants that is accompanied by the entry of large amounts of capital, the Asian languages targeted for economic reasons are also becoming major community languages. This applies not only to Chinese but also to Korean and Indonesian. There are now more speakers of Indonesian in Sydney than of Hungarian or Dutch and more speakers of Korean than of Turkish. (Japanese remains a language of temporary residents.)

It is the states that have been responsible for languages policy in recent years because school education is their prerogative. Thus there is considerable variation in languages-in-education policy, ranging from New South Wales, which requires all children to study a LOTE for at least 100 hours during their secondary education, soon to increase to 200 hours, to Victoria, which will, by 2000, require all children to take a LOTE for at least 11 years. Even the more modest policies are proving difficult to implement because of teacher shortages especially for some languages, something that is impacting on quality. Most states are ignoring Commonwealth initiatives on prioritisation. NSW and South Australia indicated priorities to the Commonwealth, for the purposes of receiving funds, but are distributing the funds for all languages. Victoria has used the priority languages as the basis for a 'balance' between European and 'Asian' languages. There are four tiers of languages (Victoria, 1984):

(1) Key languages — French, German, Italian, Modern Greek, Indonesian, Japanese, Mandarin and Vietnamese.
(2) Language for priority development — Arabic, Korean, Russian, Spanish and Thai.
(3) Language of particular significance (especially in a given geographical area) e.g. Auslan, Croatian, Hebrew, Khmer, Koorie (Aboriginal) languages, Macedonian, Maltese, Serbian, Turkish.
(4) Other languages, usually taught on Saturdays (see page 99).

Productive Diversity

An important change in Australian public policy is that multilingualism is now no longer widely perceived to be either a problem or a specific right for some groups. In an age in which economic advantage is seen as the basis for all arguments, Australia's projection of multilingualism as an economic benefit continues to provide a stimulus for languages other than English in education and beyond. Languages are now recognised as a national resource, and progressively all Australians are involved in developing existing or new language skills. Potentially, this confers a new status on bilinguals as those with economic capital rather than just underprivileged people, with the result that the individual's and the ethnic group's self-esteem and social mobility and the nation's financial interests can be reconciled. The harnessing of language resources can mutually benefit the nation and the people whose skills are under-utilised. This is in keeping with the general outlook dominated by greed and selfishness to the extent that even strong opponents of racism have felt obliged to resort to warning that racism must be halted because it is bad for our balance of trade rather than to appeal to justice and social conscience. In this climate, the notion of globalisation can strengthen how we utilise our multi-culturalism. The need to increase trade with non-English- speaking countries and the language and cultural requirements of this have been discussed in various reports. It must be stated, however, that business is divided on the value of language and cultural competence in this (see e.g. Stanley *et al.*, 1990; ALLC, 1990; Kipp *et al.*, 1995).

Much is being made of Australia's need to become fully attuned to its role in globalisation. But when you have the kinds of language resources that Australia has, when you have the kind of experience of inter-cultural communication that Australians of all kinds of backgrounds are gaining and have gained — at work, at school, on housing estates and in shopping centres — globalisation can begin at home. If utilised appropriately, the experience acquired, even at the grassroots, together with our collective resources in a wide diversity of languages, could make Australia a vital link between Europe, Asia, the Middle East and Latin America. Already many European multinational firms are establishing their Asia-Pacific headquarters in Sydney or Melbourne because they perceive Australia as a link between Europe and Asia. The notion of Productive Diversity was strongly developed by former Prime Minister, Paul Keating.

Universities in some states have espoused the argument that a knowledge of a second language is useful in all professions and are giving bonuses for entry scores on the basis of students' results in a language other than English.

The management of Australia's community language diversity will thus be of the utmost importance to this nation. This is something that can be strengthened by encouraging the maintenance *and* development of all languages and cultures where the people themselves desire it and by facilitating the utilisation of language resources and language maintenance institutions for the acquisition of the vast range of languages in use in Australia. However, there is a danger that mainstreaming is not providing this give and take.

Spreading Multilingualism

Recent research (e.g. Kipp *et al.*, 1995: 134–151) has shown the important contribution provided by families and ethnic communities, often at considerable cost to themselves. At the same time, there continues to be substantial wastage of language resources, especially in the second and third generations, as I have already mentioned. Fishman (1991: 276) comments that Australian 'policies and processes constitute a positive but ineffective approach to reversing language shift on behalf of recent immigrant languages ...'. The dilemma in a cohesive multicultural society is how much of the cohesion and the sharing you lose if you create the more secluded and insulated environment for the languages to thrive. The maintenance of languages in community situations has been shown to benefit the wider teaching of the language. For instance, a study of four second languages at primary school by students without a background in the language (Clyne *et al.*, 1995) found that the school with the best results in each language, regardless of the programme model, was the one that tapped most into community resources. This ranged from time-tabling a period a week for a visit to a nearby German- speaking old people's home, listening to and making Greek-language radio programmes, or incorporating shopping expeditions to

Italian-speaking shops. The linguistic impact of friendships with children from Chinese-speaking families made the demography of the school an important factor.

Language maintenance is cognitively advantageous to the individual, supports family cohesion, and is a cultural asset to the community and the nation. In promoting the development, transmission and sharing of multilingual resources, we must make bilinguals feel good about their bilingualism. It has been shown (Gardner & Lambert, 1972; Crookes & Schmidt, 1989; Gardner & McIntyre, 1991; Ellis, 1994: 508–17) that motivation (instrumental, integrative and intrinsic) plays a vital role in successful second language acquisition. It is also essential in successful language maintenance. Smolicz (1971) described the Australian school of the 1960s and early 1970s as 'an assimilation agent'. Do the Australian education systems of the 1990s exercise the same function, in relation to language maintenance and shift, despite a decade of national and state languages policies and despite the declaration of LOTEs as compulsory subjects in the primary and secondary schools of some states?

The introduction of a wide range of languages into the school curriculum and as Year 12 examination subjects was directed towards making it possible for young people to develop their potential to the fullest and towards legitimising all the languages of Australia. However, the new perception of languages other than English as important subjects at primary and secondary schools and their status as a key learning area have not only overstretched resources in some states to the point of diminishing standards, it has brought with it in most states a renewed set of false assumptions about whom language programmes are for. There is some feeling that students with a home background studying that language are illicitly taking something away from those who do not have such a background and their very presence in a LOTE class is deemed unfair. The 'problem' is of course greatest in Asian languages which are mostly perceived as difficult subjects and many of whose students with home backgrounds are fairly recent arrivals with a high level of competence. The issue of advantage needs to be considered in the context of 'global scores' which operate in a number of states. Thereby a student's results in a subject are related to their results in all other subjects and to all the other candidates' results in the subject upward or downward. Thus some subjects are regarded as more difficult than others and scores can be adjusted very substantially. Four state examination boards have devised LOTE forms to interrogate students on their home use of the language in order to classify them in terms of their 'advantage'. The questions relate to the frequency with which a language is heard, spoken, read and written at home or the rank ordering of languages for those purposes, as well as the amount of schooling obtained in a country where the language is spoken. Such questions are also employed to assess the disadvantage in English. In Victoria, one of the functions of these forms is to moderate the LOTE bonus for university entry, where it exists.

Some states are now offering or preparing to offer 'first language' examinations in some LOTEs and constrain admission to 'second language' examinations. As Elder (1994: 3) comments in a report on the Victorian 1994 LOTE Form, information on the relation between speaker background and performance is needed to be able to assess the need for differentiated examinations. She points out that, for instance, the candidates in Greek are generally 'less native-like' (1994: 3) than those in Chinese, but more likely to use the language at home in the second generation, more likely to have taken it at primary and secondary level, and less likely to speak a dialect. Another problem is 'global scores', which are restricting the number of outstanding results in a subject. It is important for a student starting from scratch in a language at secondary school to be able to gain the mark they deserve regardless of how competent others may be in the language. However, there is a serious danger that the casualties of the operation will be second and third generation Australians who, together with their parents and teachers, have worked hard against statistical probability to maintain the community language and develop it to a reasonable level. In many cases, only one parent speaks the language; in many, the parent/s are themselves Australian-born and do not provide a strictly 'native' model. Families have often embarked on bilingual language acquisition for the children because of their commitment to a multicultural Australia which they did not enjoy as children due to the assimilation policy at that time, and to a future for their children in a global situation. In the first generation the community language is often maintained because of a communicative need caused by limited English. In the second generation, however, it is the result of determination and often becomes a symbolic instrument of identity, especially a multiple identity. And yet the students are given the impression that they are not playing by the rules and have to be penalised for this. Forms on family background do not have to be completed by students enrolling in Information Technology about their access to computers in the home from an early age and the competence of the parents to use them, or, for students taking Music or Theatre Studies, about their exposure to music or to the theatre through the participation of the parents actively or passively in such activities.

Recent Research Projects

I would now like to report on two relevant recent projects conducted by the Language and Society Centre at Monash. The first (Clyne, 1997) is a study of a sample of upper secondary students in Victoria describing the diversity of backgrounds represented in the student body. We explored their language and the methodologies and policies adopted to cater for their needs and to address the diversity in LOTE programmes. The three languages selected for the study were Chinese (Mandarin), German, and Italian. Each of these communities represent a different stage in the history of multilingualism/multiculturalism in Australia, and the languages differ in language maintenance patterns, as well as typologically and sociolinguistically. There is a rich variation in each of the languages. In terms of mutual intelligibility Cantonese should be considered a separate language and the advantage of knowing it as a basis for Mandarin is minimal unless one is literate in it, for there is a common writing system. The incidence of monodialectism was quite common in the Southern Italian homeland when the families of the present Italian-English bilingual children came to Australia. In 1991, 18.1% of Mandarin speakers and 19.1% of Cantonese speakers but only 10.8% of Italian speakers and 7.4% of German speakers in Australia were in the 0–14 age group.

Categorisation of Learners

The assumption that there are two easily definable groups — home background and non-background students — or even three easily definable groups of students — in the LOTE classroom is somewhat misguided. Most generally fall somewhere between L1 and L2 speakers of the language, on the whole different from either but clustering more at the L2 end of the continuum. There is a wide diversity of students who did not begin secondary school LOTE classes as beginners. They include:

(1)   Ethnic background learners:
  (1.1) Recent arrivals with the target language as principal or sole language of socialisation and cognitive development as well as medium of school instruction at secondary school.
  (1.2) Less recent arrivals with a strong background in the language who have attended school in a country where it is spoken. Some have had most or all of their primary education in that country, others frequently commute between Australia and the country of origin.
  (1.3) Those who start school with a good knowledge of the spoken language which may or may not be developed further.
  (1.4) Those with a colloquial home background which suffices for vital family communication but is very limited in lexicon, grammar and style due to its restricted range of uses.
  (1.5) Those with a passive knowledge of the spoken language only, for example, those whose parents speak the language to each other but not to the child(ren). *In many ethnolinguistic communities, this constitutes the majority of the younger generation.*
  (1.6) Those with a limited active and passive knowledge of the language, based on direct input addressed to the child by only one parent and/or one or more grandparents. The children may therefore lack indirect input, i.e. overhearing other interactions in the language. Such limited exposure and the limited number of interlocutors distinguish such language acquirers from normal 'native speakers'. This category usually results from a deliberate decision to 'keep the language going' in far from optimum conditions.
  (1.7) Those speaking a variety so strongly influenced by English that, while adequate for everyday communication in Australia, it does not adhere to 'native' norms and may not be readily comprehensible to monolingual speakers of the language.

In each of the categories (1.3) to (1.7), the language to which the student has been exposed may be a regional or local variety that is socially stigmatised and very different from the variety of the classroom and examination.

(2)   Non-ethnic background learners:
  (2.1) Those who have spent time living and attending school in a country

where the language is spoken, thereby being exposed to the culture and to the four language skills. Their competence will be influenced by variables such as length of time in the country, level of schooling and the circumstances of the visit.

(2.2) Children raised bilingually by parents or a parent who had acquired the language as a foreign language.

(2.3) Those exposed to the target language at primary school: in varying extents according to the number of years of target language study, time on task, and the type of programme (e.g. immersion or content based, language object, satellite only) (Clyne *et al.*, 1997: 5–9).

Only the category (1.1) is clear-cut; there is no dividing line between the others; there is a lot of overlap, with intermediate categories, and some of the categories under (2) have the same tangible results as those under (1.3) or (1.6) (Strong communicative competence but weaker grammatical competence and much English influence). The only category that can be defined for a separate examination is (1.1).

Where all the input in the language comes from one parent, it is direct, i.e. directed to the child, who receives little or no indirect input, such as overhearing adults use the language, which provides models for interaction. Other limitations in the background of young people speaking a community language in Australia are:

(1) The model to which they are exposed may not adhere to 'native' norms; it may be reduced, simplified and/or strongly influenced by English. This is particularly the case of the parent(s) born or attending school in Australia.

(2) Unless the children receive some component of bilingual education, the input will be highly context-embedded.

(3) The students are not part of a situation in which the language is used in a full range of domains and uses. Also, young people in Australia often do not take advantage of input and output opportunities where these are available because they occur outside the social networks to which they belong or wish to belong. On the whole, radio programmes, ethnic newspapers and social clubs and even TV programmes are considered of little or no interest by the younger generation (cf. also Clyne & Kipp, 1997).

(4) The students lack the corrective element provided by the media, adult conversation, school subjects taught through the medium of the language, and a peer group interacting in the language. These would enable children in 'native' settings to modify the effects of natural acquisition processes and prevent ungrammatical forms from becoming fossilised.

Thus, this context provides less than optimal conditions for the development of language in terms of:

(a) Comprehensible input which enables the acquirer to develop grammatical hypotheses and confirm them through more input, direct feedback or communicative breakdown.

(b) Output opportunities to practise and check the hypotheses.

(c) Communicative need (i.e. need to use the language in communicative situations),
(d) Functional specialisation between the languages.

In-country experience can effect changes in this, especially among those who already have some competence in the language. This facilitates integrative motivation, provides strong communicative needs, input and output opportunities, constant exposure to standard norms, stimulating the modification of grammatical hypotheses and the acquisition of pragmatic formulae. The strong base in the community language that some children developed prior to migration to Australia was soon eroded by the need to acquire English quickly. However, first generation bilinguals who regularly visit the country of origin are able to constantly refresh and develop their language. How durable the effect of such visits are in the second generation depends on their length and frequency and whether the language is spoken at home by the parents. While home use means that the momentum can be kept up, transference may set in again soon after their return because of the exigencies of the environment and the parents' own speech patterns. Those within the category termed 'ethnic background' tend to have native-like pronunciations but not necessarily a high level of grammatical competence. Those who answer in English at home develop very good receptive skills and tend not to exhibit the same level of communicative competence or as native-like pronunciation as those who speak the language at home. In both categories, however, there is uncertainty as to the meaning of words, due to the restricted contexts in which the language is used, but considerable creativity. Though there is overlap, e.g. between the second generation and young first generation, our German data confirm Gonzo and Saltarelli's (1983) model of grammatical simplification across generations, especially in relation to the overgeneralisation of *das* and of *den* across genders, overgeneralisation of 'have' as auxiliary, *es* as a pronoun reference for inanimate as a natural gender, and, to some extent, the replacement of pragmatic by grammatical word order (also Clyne, 1997). Orthography is subject to simplification processes and the transference of English patterns due to a time lag between the acquisition of the spoken and written modes of the language and the impact of English-medium schools.

Many young Italo-Australians are from Calabrian and Sicilian families who were dialect-speaking. The distance between the dialect and the Standard Italian required in classroom and assessment is great. Their exposure to Standard Italian outside school is too limited for the simultaneous development of two varieties. As the Italian link is basically with extended family and the elderly family friends network, the inter-regional ethnic functions and the Italo-Australian media are of little interest to them. They have not been shown how to build a competence in Standard Italian from their competence in their dialect. In the context of a substantial shift to English in the family, any ongoing symbolic linguistic code is more likely to be an Italian ethnolect of Australian English (Cavallaro, 1997). This means that the potential resource, exemplified especially in the excellent listening comprehension of the students, is destroyed by an inferiority complex and frequent denigration through the school system, even though the introduction of Italian as a school subject — still the most widely taught language in primary school and the most widely taught languages in Catholic schools — was motivated by its importance as the community language of the largest non-English-speaking ethnic group.

Children who had participated in primary school programmes especially content- based ones exhibit some features shared with second generation bilinguals — excellent receptive skills, very good communicative competence, and low grammatical competence. However, high grammatical competence was quite usual for many from non-ethnic backgrounds who had had in-country study experience. And we need to differentiate between structurally oriented learners, with an interest in linguistic structures, and functionally-oriented learners, who are merely interested in getting a message across (Nicholas, 1984).

The Chinese section of the study displayed some marked differences from that of the other two languages. Among the differences is the much larger first generation, particularly young people who had received a considerable part of their education overseas, with a correspondingly small second and no third generation maintaining the language and taking matriculation examinations in Mandarin. The other factors peculiar to Chinese include the mutual unintelligibility of Mandarin and other *fangyan*, notably Cantonese, at least in their spoken mode, and the comparatively large amount of time required for a non-native speaker to acquire the language. Thus, we see here the considerable attrition of skills and fossilised development related to increased length of residence in Australia and a set of problems, particularly in phonology and tones but also in grammar (e.g. aspect markers, classifiers) and the lexicon, of Cantonese speakers acquiring Mandarin. As in the case of Italian, the grandparents tend to speak non-standard varieties and they are the ones who provide the cultural and linguistic continuity as the family establishes itself in Australia. The problems of Chinese literacy are particularly great as the Cantonese speakers are thought to be advantaged but only benefit from their background in the other *fangyan* if they first become literate in it before learning Mandarin.

Before I discuss some of our suggestions for dealing with the situation, let me refer to Valdès (1995), who has considered this from an American, especially Hispanic-American viewpoint. He argues that theories of applied linguistics should be applied to the field of teaching Spanish to hispanophone bilinguals. Valdès develops typologies of needs for first and later generations. First generation children should continue to develop age-appropriate competencies, develop L1 literacy skills, and acquire the prestige variety of the language. The second and third generations should maintain, retrieve and/or acquire language competencies, expand their bilingual range, transfer skills acquired in either language, and acquire the prestige variety of the language (Valdès, 1995: 307). He suggests less frequently used pedagogies such as introducing sociolinguistic principles of language variation and language use, participatory activities to expand sociolinguistic and pragmatic as well as grammatical competence, consciousness-raising about issues of language and identity, and the conduct of ethnographic community projects (Valdès, 1995: 309).

There are a number of general issues that have recurred across languages in the study. Firstly, the big distinction is between those who have recently arrived after receiving at least some major part of their secondary education in a country where the language is used as a national language and medium of instruction. This is the only objective criterion of differentiation. Most categories of students are advantaged only in some areas of the target language. They have resources that need to be developed and needs that have to be addressed. Moreover, they have to be motivated like other learners of the language. If their language maintenance efforts are denigrated, they will justifiably feel cheated.

Underlying much of the current assessment policy is the fallacy of the 'double monolingual'. In an educational climate where there is a great deal of pressure on LOTE teachers, the generic syllabus and assumption of the homogenous class are the least trouble. Yet, it is enrichment options that will enable students with 'backgrounds', whether ethnic or non-ethnic ones, to build on their resource and do something extra, thus dissipating the perception of a need for intrusive forms. We are also proposing special materials for the various categories of students, to be developed nationally for classroom use, distance education and self-instruction using new technologies. These resources would focus on the relevant grammatical or orthographic problems and on areas of lexical transference. We are also suggesting the development of materials for teachers in Italian and Chinese similar to the German series *Dialekt- Hochsprache-Kontrastiv* (Besch *et al.*, 1977) to equip teachers to understand questions of variation among the dialect or non-Mandarin speakers and to use the dialect or *fangyan* as a resource for competence in that dialect and Standard, or the *fangyan* and Mandarin. Moreover, we believe consideration should be given to the addition of Cantonese to the list of examinable subjects.

In terms of classroom practice, we observed the situation in a number of schools teaching the relevant languages. Although there was some sympathy for the issue concerned, very few attempts had been made to motivate the students with family backgrounds in the language, especially where this is limited. Such attempts have included peer group tutoring, extra grammatical exercises and book reviews. There were fewer examples of acceleration to higher levels than in areas such as Mathematics or Drama/Theatre Studies, and no instances of opportunities to let students utilise their knowledge of the language and culture to enhance other subjects. Among less helpful practices were focusing on background speakers' weaknesses in grammar and ignoring their communicative competence, and developing assessment systems which reward non-background learners, while penalising limited-background students. The three tenets of an unfortunate 'us-them' dichotomy are:

(1) That the 'background learners' have an unfair advantage and are getting something for nothing.
(2) That they are unteachable.
(3) That their language competence does not need to be developed, only maintained until the others catch up.

I stress that the self-esteem and confidence of those without a background in the language must not be undermined by the myth that they will always be disadvantaged. There is much opportunity in multicultural Australia of sharing languages. While some have more competence in a language, others have the distance from which they can reflect on the language. Vertical classes in languages as well as the use of new technologies and community resources might be a good start. This will mean making the the sacred time-table much more flexible! The very impressive performance of those who have had in-country school experience indicates that this is an opportunity everyone should have. Content-based programmes employing immersion techniques have the advantage of being able to accommodate students from a range of backgrounds and those without a background in the language, because of the emphasis on content learning, opportunities for links with other subject areas, for learning at your own pace and peer group tutoring, and the acquisition of special registers for certain subject areas. They offer the four essential ingredients of good second language programmes mentioned earlier. However, this is possible only with adequate time on-task and sufficient emphasis on language development, as we found in another project (Clyne *et al.*, 1995).

Raising Children Bilingually

The sad thing is that it is those with limited background and who put much effort into maintaining and developing the language, the second and third generation, who seem to be hardest hit in the 'us and them' dichotomy. This is in the context of a widespread but not always very well informed effort at language maintenance in the interests of the next generation. The Australian literature on raising children bilingually (e.g. Saunders, 1982, 1988; Döpke, 1993) has used empirical studies to indicate to parents successful means of achieving it. Participation in weekend seminars conducted over the years by the Monash-based Language and Society Centre of the National Languages and Literacy Institute of Australia has demonstrated the enthusiasm for bilingual language acquisition and the effort that people are putting into it, especially in the third generation, where only one parent is bilingual. Grandparents, especially grandmothers, are now playing a vital role in this as the caregivers of young children during the working week. The enthusiasm with which they have taken on the transmission of the community language to the grandchildren is often motivated by the desire to compensate for the less successful maintenance of the language in the second generation during a period of less favourable community attitudes.

Even more opportunities are needed for information exchange between parents, teachers and caregivers, researchers and others, and the many who assume several of these roles in the transmission and management of linguistic diversity. The multicultural and ethnic media could be doing a great deal more to provide suitable and appropriate input for language acquisition, maintenance and development for the young in programmes that are of interest to them. In so doing they would also be guaranteeing their own future. The current discussion on assessment of LOTE students seems to be focused on the 'problem' of difference; it ignores the efforts and aspirations of Australians wishing to pass on to their children a gift of their multiculturalism as a contribution to their lives in a globalised, tolerant society, it neglects the needs of the young people whose strengths and weaknesses are different to those of beginners. These are completely different categories to those who have recently arrived with a substantial education in the country of origin.

Some Policy Suggestions Concerning Diversity in LOTE Programmes

Our study has led us to question the wisdom of global scores, which is a more general issue. The practice of intrusive forms should, in our view, be stopped unless they are required for all subject areas. They are totally inadequate for the purposes for which they are intended as they do not give any indication of the nature and extent of the input available and only convey the impression that language maintenance is something that will get you into trouble. With the current pressure on teachers, coping with diversity in the LOTE classroom is an additional burden. Vertical time-tables, allowing the kinds of accelerated programmes facilitated for Mathematics, the Sciences and the Arts, together with the full gamut of possibilities, including the use of the internet, e- mail, overseas satellite and other technological advances should be adopted. Beyond that, it is largely a matter of pooling resources. Long before multicultural policies, many young Australians developed native-like competence in languages other then English from their neighbours and friends. This is continuing today, and something that needs to be encouraged on a larger basis. This requires collaboration between ethnic communities and education systems. The use of peer group support is all the more advantageous because it is from the background categories that we can expect some motivated young people to come to fill the largely empty ranks of language teachers when the implementation of state language policies requires more and more.

Activation and Reactivation

Any list of language shift rates will show the substantial proportion of people who have a background in a community language which they do not use or do not use much today. This includes people who have effectively lost their skills in the language or who have only passive skills in it. Part of utilising language resources is finding out more about the process of reactivating lost skills and activating passive ones. Ammerlaan (1996) provides some insights into this issue. He examines the L1 attrition and retrieval processes of Dutch speakers in Australia and the role of interlingual identification between Dutch and English. Dutch words, he finds, have not vanished from people's memory but their recall has slowed down, the non-use of Dutch having affected Dutch lexical processing rather than language knowledge. Recovery and activation programmes cutting the acquisition process would thus be feasible and a time and money saver. In addition, they could provide a basis for similar work among second language acquirers who are resuming the learning of a language after a time lag.

The Second Project

I said earlier that we had chosen the three languages largely because they represented different stages in the multicultural history of Australia. The Chinese of tomorrow will go through the same process as the German and Italian of today and so will the Korean and Indonesian of the day after tomorrow. This issue is a recurrent one, and the actual languages will vary. Let me now draw on another project, which Sandra Kipp and I have recently completed, with the help of some colleagues at the University of Western Sydney (Stuart Campbell, Bruno di Biase and Rosemary Suleiman). We were looking at how three new community languages, all languages of wider communication and economic significance, all pluricentric languages, were being maintained. The project had both quantitative and qualitative components. One section of the project considered taking language maintenance of the community language as a subject in Year 12 (the last year of schooling). For each of the languages we chose two countries of origin — Egypt and Lebanon for Arabic, Chile and Spain for Spanish, Hong Kong and Taiwan for Chinese, and, of course, in the case of the Hong Kong group, the Mandarin that was taken at school was, in effect, a different language from the Cantonese they spoke at home. This means that Cantonese was a strong language of identity with more limited market-place value in contrast to Mandarin which to most of the Taiwanese had both functions. The market-place value of English, together with reactions to prejudice, have led to decline in the interest for Chinese. In the case of the Arabic speakers, the Muslims have a stronger language maintenance motivation than the Christians because to the former, Arabic is the language of God. Increasingly Arabic is a symbol of an Arabic-Australian identity which transcends country of origin. This is weaker among Maronites and Copts than among some other groups. Promoting Arabic language and culture in the wider community was seen as an antidote to prejudice. There was an interactive relation in all the groups between the choice of Year 12 language subject, language proficiency, and attitudes to the language. Those studying the language in which they have a background as a Year 12 subject generally came from homes in which the language is used more, and they tended to differentiate it more strongly from English in form and function. But taking the subject enhanced the development of, and confidence in, their language proficiency and their literacy in the language, which were greater than those of the same age and educational level not taking the language as a subject. Those taking the language as a subject had stronger attitudes towards the advantages of bilingualism, the desirability of the maintenance of ethnicity and the vital role of language in this. The only group that showed considerable anxiety about the present assessment procedures were the Chinese speakers. They are the group who had already experienced separate examinations and the Cantonese speakers in particular felt discriminated against. These issues will probably become more important in the second and third generations.

Languages and the Future of Multiculturalism in Australia

So far I may have depicted a rather negative situation which contrasts with a widespread view that Australia was some kind of multicultural utopia and a model for pluralistic language policies. Was that an illusion or has there been a complete reversal? Are we seeing the end of the idyll? How bad are things really and, if they are, what has motivated the change? Is it new racism or economic fear or what?

First of all, let me say that Australia is a multicultural society — that is a demographic reality. There is no English Only legislation, no burning down of migrant hostels, people are not now abused in trams or over the fence for speaking languages other than English; there are still institutions to enable people who wish to maintain community languages to do so. And if there are racist incidents, there can be appeal to a Human Rights and Equal Opportunity Commission. For most Australians, multiculturalism is part of their national identity and a fact of life. This is so particularly in the younger and middle generations, and less so in the older generation, and in rural areas of the outlying states, Queensland and Western Australia. Commitment to multiculturalism has varied between different states of Australia since the early days of colonisation and appears to be related to settlement patterns. This has been reflected in innovative approaches to multicultural education originating in South Australia and Victoria (Clyne,1991: 7–11, 25–27). Also, the whole of Australian history has been marked by a tension between monolingualism/monoculturalism and multilingualism/multiculturalism. I am of the firm belief that the latter is now quite secure in Australia. Whenever there appears to be any threat to one of the institutions of multiculturalism, the politician or planner seen to be making this suggestion has to retract it due to the opposition not only of ethnic groups but also, particularly, of the open-minded mainstream and their mouthpieces, the Australian Broadcasting Corporation and quality newspapers such as Melbourne's *The Age* and the *Sydney Morning Herald*. This has happened consistently over the years, whether the issue has been multicultural TV, radio scheduling, school programmes or the whole concept of multiculturalism. A recent example of a challenge and reversal is a statement by the new Chair of the Victorian Board of Studies (schools examinations board), Professor Kwong Lee Dow, reportedly favouring a drastic reduction in the number of languages examined, due to very low numbers in some languages (*The Age*, 27 February 1997). This was followed by an immediate retraction by the State Minister for Education and a joint statement by the minister and the chair of the Board of Studies extolling the virtues of teaching many languages (*The Age*, 28 February 1997). In December 1994, following complaints, the State Premier intervened to prevent a component of the assessment in eight languages from not being counted because too many students obtained (A) or (A+) in it. The Board of Studies had argued that the problem was due to home users of a language being assessed on the criteria of students without a background (Richards, 1993).

There are three major political factors that might explain why unprecedented support for and valuing of languages other than English have evidently been accompanied by a change for the worse: the general espousal of economic rationalism, an educational explosion in a basically utilitarian and anti- intellectual society, and the problems of defining advantage and disadvantage in a self-described 'classless' society. There is a close interaction between these factors. As I mentioned above, during the shift from assimilation to multiculturalism, language maintenance institutions such as community languages in schools and ethnic schools, libraries, interpreting, community language radio and TV, became the financial responsibility of the state. This was part of mainstreaming multiculturalism. But now many of the former state responsibilities, from hospitals to prisons, from public transport to gas and electricity and telecommunications, are being privatised. Increasingly, things operate on user-pays principles. Nothing in the mainstream is escaping. It is natural that language maintenance institutions will also be affected although the extent of this has not yet been contemplated. Neither the common good nor the rights of the underprivileged are now necessarily the concern of governments. Students' higher education contributions are being increased, in some cases steep university fees are being introduced and making money is replacing teaching and research as the function of the university; schools are being closed, the budget of the Australian Broadcasting Corporation is being slashed, Radio Australia and TV Australia have been threatened with closure or privatisation. The Bureau of Immigration, Multicultural and Population Research has been closed, but so have other research bodies. Migrants with less than two years' residence in Australia will now not be eligible for social services (this does not apply to refugees) and the unemployed will have to work for their dole.

The negative association of the 'advantaged' migrant has a historical basis. There were two main reasons for the post-war mass immigration programme — the expansion of secondary industry, which required 'factory fodder' and the widespread belief, following the Japanese bombing of Darwin, that Australia had to 'populate or perish', i.e. it had to take on large numbers of European migrants in order to stave off the 'hoards from Asia' wanting to 'take over Australia'. During the next decades integration occurred through what might be termed the Escalator Effect. As a new group became part of the Australian mosaic, it entered at the bottom of the socio-economic escalator and all the existing groups moved up. In most cases, the new groups were more different and distant from the 'mainstream' than the earlier ones. All this changed with the new categorisation of migrant intake — comprising family reunion, humanitarian, business and special skills categories. The business migrants, in particular, a category devised in keeping with the ethos of the 1980s, entered at the top rather than the bottom of the escalator. Whereas previously even very well qualified refugees had to 'make it' back into their former social status gradually via the factory floor, the business migrants seemed to be advantaged right from the beginning and did not enable anyone else to move one step up on the escalator. In fact, this was a time of high unemployment. That the new migrants were actually creating jobs for other Australians was not considered by some people. The problem was that the business migrants tended to be from Hong Kong and Taiwan and the succession of post-war migrants had now reached the point where the East Asians were the natural succession of the migration intended to protect Australia from them! The question of LOTE examination assessment policies relates to all this because there is a perception in some quarters that 'too many' of the students who gain admission into prestigious faculties are of Asian background and that they may be helped by being able to count 'their language'. This is strange, considering that Australia is trying to woo large numbers of international students from Asia in order to offset substantial spending cuts on universities. It is not taken into account that some cultures consider scholarship and effort in learning to be more crucial than others as a value and an achievement. Every now and then, people (mainly of the older generation) with racist views come out of the woodwork and generate a phase of racist discourse in the community. This is an indication that the tension between monoculturalism and multiculturalism is still extant beneath the surface. It is, however, not an indication of a change in Australian attitude. Phases of this kind occurred, for example, in 1984, when a historian, Professor Geoffrey Blainey conducted a public campaign against Asian migration and against multiculturalism in general. There were many instances reported to the Human Rights and Equal Opportunity Commission of racial vilification or discrimination against Arabs and Muslims about the time of the Gulf War.

It is sometimes difficult to distinguish between genuine debates on restrictions on the level of immigration other than the humanitarian category and outright racism. However, racism against Asians is frequently combined with even more vicious utterances against indigenous Australians in relation to the controversy on whether pastoral leases should extinguish native titles. Unambiguous instances have been clearly initiated by two Independent Members of Federal Parliament, Graeme Campbell, who represents a mining and pastoral electorate in Western Australia and who was expelled from the Labor Party for racism and association with a far-right group, and Pauline Hanson who, having been disowned by the Liberal Party for anti-Aboriginal statements, was subsequently elected to represent a provincial Queensland town with a large working-class vote.

Whenever there is a situation of this kind, quick action by government and other leaders is required to calm the situation and balance media inclinations to exaggerate the issue. This had always been done by prime ministers Whitlam, Fraser, Hawke, and Keating as well as by several state premiers, where any need arose. Hanson's repetitive racist remarks were unanimously rejected by Federal Parliament on 30 October 1996 in a declaration in favour of racial harmony, Aboriginal reconciliation, and continuing non-discriminatory immigration policy, moved by the Prime Minister and seconded by the Leader of the Opposition, following a debate from which Hanson chose to absent herself and Campbell abstained. A similar declaration supporting racial tolerance and cultural diversity was accepted unanimously by the Victorian state parliament. The Governor-General, Sir William Deane, declared multiculturalism to be 'the basis of our nation'. The qualities of tolerance and defending the rights of the less fortunate, he said, 'have manifested themselves in the way we have built one of the most culturally diverse but harmonious societies in the world' (*The Age*, 9 December 1996: 4). However, it is unfortunate that the Prime Minister, John Howard, was slow to react and, in what he sees as a plea for a return to freedom of speech and an attack on what he calls 'political correctness', has championed a change in the discourse of disadvantage and difference.

> There is no doubt one of the second or third order reasons why the Labor Party lost the last election was the growing feeling of frustration amongst a lot of people that we had become too politically correct. There was too much social censorship, it was impossible to talk about certain issues without being smeared with the tag of racist or extremist or sexist on this or that. (*The Age* June 1996: 17)

The slogan, 'For all of us' (used by the Liberal party in the election which they went on to win) though misunderstood by many voters, marked the beginning of an era in which the disadvantaged — especially when perceived as 'different' — whether indigenous, women, immigrants, unemployed or homosexuals — are accused of having had it too good. Just as the word 'reform' has internationally undergone a semantic shift from changes in the direction of social equity to changes in the direction of economic rationalism, there is a reversal in the meaning of the 'privileged'. This is relevant to the discussion of students with a home background in a language insofar as many come from socioeconomically deprived backgrounds and their bilingualism has often been a route to educational advancement, especially if they could overcome the 'disadvantage' of their non-standard home variety.

Whenever cutbacks occur, they affect indigenous groups first and foremost. The above changes are no exception, in the continuing controversies surrounding land rights and Aboriginal involvement in decision-making on their own affairs. Some members of the government are not reluctant to make insensitive remarks about indigenous Australians and the Prime Minister has refused to contradict publicly statements by people like Hanson, in the interests of freedom of speech. As a former Victorian premier, John Cain said at a well-attended rally against racism in Melbourne on 8 December 1996, 'Freedom of speech is not a licence'. Incidentally, Mr Howard is also attempting to reintroduce gender exclusive language, including the term 'chairman' as a male generic.

Over the past few decades, Australia, like many other countries, has experienced an educational explosion, with substantial increases in school retention rates up to Year 12 and in participation in university education. On the whole this is making for a better informed population. The present government, however, is drawing on a strong anti-intellectual tradition in Australia, by identifying 'political correctness with intellectual elites divorced from the views of the population at large or 'broad community values' (*The Age*, 6 July 1996: 5). This contrasts with the position of the previous Prime Minister, Paul Keating, who, while advocating a free market economy and economic rationalism, also strongly pushed a human rights agenda with multiculturalism and reconciliation with the indigenous population as major tenets, particularly in the context of an imminent Australian Republic, an issue that the new government has put on slow track. Keating formalised the notion of Australian citizenship entailing both rights and obligations. The first right was 'to expressing and sharing of individual cultural heritage, including language and religion'. The obligations included 'Loyalty to Australia, its interests and future' followed by the acceptance of various overarching principles of Australian society, linking the various cultural groups, including English as a national language (NOT official language), alongside the Constitution, parliamentary democracy, freedom of speech and religion, and equality of the sexes (*The Age*, 27 April 1995). This concurs with the recommendations of the World Commission on Culture and Development in their report, Our Creative Diversity (WCCD, 1994: 16–17) which regards pluralism as basic and prefers to see a nation as a civic community rooted in shared values. While the Labor Government set Australia on the path to economic rationalism, privatisation and corporatisation, and strongly advocated links with Asia, even to the downgrading of those with Europe, the federal Liberal-National Party coalition (and especially its Prime Minister) is dominated by a hankering after the 1950s. At that time, there was a semblance of harmony and cohesion with everyone knowing their place in society. It seems that the present Prime Minister does not see it as his role to provide leadership on issues of national direction and rather waits for some kind of national consensus to develop.

Multiculturalism and Economic Rationalism

Can multiculturalism and economic rationalism mix? I find it hard to imagine how economic rationalism can mix with any principles of human dignity or intellectual progress. Nevertheless there are some, such as the present Premier and Minister for Multicultural Affairs of Victoria, the populist Jeff Kennett, from the same side of politics as John Howard, who are championing both multi-culturalism and extreme forms of economic rationalism. I would argue that it is only within the context of a truly multicultural society that economic advantage will be derived from our language resources. If the utilisation of language and cultural resources is seen as an economic asset in the context of globalisation and free markets, then it is possible to 'do business' with economic rationalists but this can be done only through a proactive programme of civil society.

Towards a National Strategy for Managing Language Diversity

I believe that in countries such as Australia a national strategy needs to be worked out within an ongoing comprehensive national languages policy, for the management of linguistic diversity, in the interests of individuals, families, communities, and especially the nation. This should involve the education systems, teachers, educational institutions, the ethnic communities, and the multicultural and ethnic media and also some informed and sympathetic members of the business community. The strategy should aim to cooperatively formulate and implement co-operatively ways of developing the nation's rich multilingual resources to the common good, and to provide language and cultural resources for language maintenance and development, for second language acquisition and development, for the activation of lost skills and for the reactivation of passivised ones. It would involve harnessing community re-sources and print and electronic media, as well as new technologies linking Australia with the linguistic heartlands and immigrant communities in other countries to assist the plan. The strategy would seek to make bi- or multi-lingualism achievable and pleasurable for all young people, taking into account their backgrounds and needs. It would include a national project for the development of study materials for the diverse groups of students with some kind of background in the language they are taking. Such a concerted effort would not be a novelty for Australia. It had its precedent in the development of the national languages policy which was described by the Australian political scientist and writer Donald Horne as 'a blueprint for change ... stamped by the voice of ordinary citizens' (Horne, 1994: 19).

While in this day and age such initiatives must again come from the grassroots, all this should be seen as part of the ongoing development of language policy in Australia. This has been very much a bipartisan matter. So much depends on supporters of multilingualism initiatives to keep pressure on all parties to maintain or reinstate and keep renewing their comprehensive languages policy based on the 'English PLUS' guiding principles of the original Senate Committee (Senate, 1984).

The questions I have raised and the context, I believe, apply internationally. As the political and economic focuses change, we need to ensure that positive and wholesome developments are salvaged and that, even if we cannot keep everything, we must ensure that we can hold on to the most important advances we have achieved.

Acknowledgments

I am grateful to Leslie Bodi and Sue Wright for helpful comments, and to Ruth Arber, Murray Goot and Andrew Markus for helping me find references.

References

AILF (1993) *Australian Indigenous Languages Framework*. Adelaide: Australian Indigenous Languages Framework Project.

ALLC (1990) *Speaking About Business. Report to Australian Language and Literacy Council.* Canberra: Australian Government Publishing Service.

Ammerlaan, T. (1996) *'You Get a Bit Wobbly ...'. Exploring Bilingual Lexical Retrieval Processes in the Context of First Language Attrition.* (Dr. Litt. dissertation, University of Nijmegen). Enschede: Copy Print.

Besch, W., Löffler, H. and Reich, H.H. (1977) *Dialekt/Hochsprache-Kontrastiv.* Düsseldorf: Schwann.

Broeder, P., Extra, G., Habreken, M., van Hout, R. and Keurentjes, H. (1993) *Taalgebruik als indicator van ethniciteit.* Tilburg: Tilburg University Press.

Cavallaro, F. (1997) The language dynamics of the Italian community in Australia. Unpublished PhD. Thesis, Monash University.

Clyne, M. (1991) *Community Languages: The Australian Experience.* Cambridge: Cambridge University Press.

Clyne, M. (1997) The German of third generation bilinguals in Australia. In W. Wölck and A. de Houwer (eds) *Recent Studies on Language Contact and Language Conflict* (pp. 36–43). Bonn: Dummler.

Clyne, M., Fernandez, S., Chen, I. and Summo-O'Connell, R. (1997) *Background Speakers: Diversity in LOTE Programs and its Management.* Canberra: Language Australia.

Clyne, M., Jenkins, C., Chen, I., Tsokalidou, R. and Wallner, T. (1995) *Developing Second Language from Primary School.* Canberra: National Languages and Literacy Institute of Australia.

Clyne, M. and Kipp, S. (1995) The extent of community language maintenance in Australia. *People and Place* 3, 4–8.

Clyne, M. and Kipp, S. (1996) Language maintenance and language shift in Australia, 1991. *Australian Review of Applied Linguistics* 19, 1–19.

Clyne, M. and Kipp, S. (1997) Language maintenance in multicultural Australia. Report to the Department of Immigration and Multicultural Affairs.

Crookes, G. and R. Schmidt (1989) Motivation: Reopening the research agenda. *University of Hawaii Papers in ESL* 8, 217–56.

Dawkins, J. (1991) *Australia's Language: The Australian Language and Literacy Policy.* Canberra: Australian Government Publishing Service.

Döpke, S. (1993) *One Parent, One Language — an Interactional Approach.* Benjamins: Amsterdam.

Elder, C. (1994) VTAC Form L (LOTE Information Form). Report to the VTAC. Parkville: University of Melbourne.

Ellis, R. (1994) *The Study of Second Language Acquisition.* Oxford: Oxford University Press.

Fishman, J.A. (1988) English only — its ghosts, myths and dangers. *International Journal of the Sociology of Language* 74, 125–40.

Fishman, J.A. (1991) *Reversing Language Shift.* Clevedon: Multilingual Matters.

Gardner, R.C. and Lambert, W.E. (1972) *Attitudes and Motivation in Second Language Learning*. Newbury House: Rowley.

Gardner, R.C. and McIntyre, P. (1991) An instrumental motivation in language study: Who says it isn't effective? *Studies in Second Language Acquisition* 13, 57–72.

Gonzo, S. and Saltarelli, M. (1983) Pidginization and linguistic change in emigrant languages. In R. Andersen (ed.) *Pidginization and Creolization as Language Acquisition* (pp. 181–97). Rowley: Newbury House.

Horne, D. (1994) Teaching our youth to be Australians. *Montage* 20, August 1994, 19–20.

Kipp, S., Clyne, M. and Pauwels, A. (1995) *Immigration and Australia's Language Resources*. Canberra: Australian Government Publishing Service.

Lo Bianco, J. (1987) *National Policy on Languages*. Canberra: Australian Government Publishing Service.

Lo Bianco, J. (1997) *National Literacy Policy*. Report to the Minister for Schools, Vocational Training and Employment.

Li Wei (1994) *Three Generations, Two Languages, One Family: Language Choice and Language Shift in a Chinese Community in Britain*. Clevedon: Multilingual Matters.

Nicholas, H. (1984) Contextually defined queries: Evidence for variation in orientation to second language acquisition processes. Paper presented to the 9th Conference of the Applied Linguistic Assocation of Australia, Alice Springs.

Pauwels, A. (1995) Linguistics practices and language maintenance among women and men in Australia. *Nordlyd* 11, 21–50.

Peddie, R. (1993) From Policy to Practice: The implementation of language policies in Victoria. Report to the New Zealand Ministry of Education. University of Auckland.

Richards, C. (1993) Scores too high in some subjects, say unis. *The Age*, 16 December 1993, 41.

Rudd, K.M. (1994) *Asian Languages and Australia's Economic Future*. Canberra: Australian Government Publishing Service.

Saunders, G. (1982) *Bilingual Children — A Guide for Parents*. Clevedon: Multilingual Matters.

Saunders, G. (1988) *Bilingual Children from Birth to Teens*. Clevedon: Multilingual Matters.

Senate (1984) *National Language Policy*. Canberra: Australian Government Publishing Service.

Smolicz, J.J. (1971) Is the Australian School an assimilation agency? *Education News* 13 (4), 4–8.

Smolicz, J.J. *et al.*, (1984) *Education for a Cultural Democracy*. Adelaide: Task Force to investigate Multiculturalism and Education.

Smolicz, J.J., Lee, L., Murugaian, M. and Secombe, M.J. (1989–90) Language as a core value of culture among tertiary students of Chinese and Indian origin in Australia. *Journal of Asian Pacific Communication* 1.

Stanley, J., Ingram, D. and Chittick, G. (1990) The relationship between international trade and linguistic competence. *Report to DEET*. Canberra: Australian Government Publishing Service.

Valdès, G. (1995) The teaching of minority languages as academic subjects: Pedagogical and theoretical challenges. *The Modern Languages Journal* 79, 299–328.

Victoria (1984) *Ministerial Policy Statement 6*. Curriculum Development and Planning. Victoria: Ministry of Education.

WCCD (1994) *Our Creative Diversity*. Report of the World Commission on Culture and Diversity. Paris: UNESCO.

The Debate

Ruth Hansford (CILT): I was interested to see that Australia experiences no difficulty in including language questions in its census. What was the case made for their inclusion and has there been resistance to them? In the UK we are trying to make a business case for some kind of language question on our census. Do you have any advice about how we should go about doing this?

Michael Clyne (Monash University): We started this in 1976. It was relatively easy in the political climate at that time to ask such questions, although it would be more difficult now. However, then there was a consensus that Adult English and School Community Language Programs should be available as well as other services like translation and interpreting. The authorities needed to know the likely numbers of users of such services; there was very little resistance to asking the population.

Ruth Hansford: What were the questions on that early census?

Michael Clyne: Australians were asked what languages they used regularly and to rate their ability in these languages. In the 1986, 1991 and 1996 censuses, people were asked if they spoke a language other than English and, if so, to name the language(s). Asking what language is spoken in the home is quite misleading because it presupposes a family home with a homogenous language group in the house. This is not always the case. Many people live alone. For example, we have numerous students and young people living away from home who have no contact with speakers of their first language. In such a situation, asking what language is spoken in the home has no meaning — and yet all of these respondents ought to contribute to the statistics which show the language diversity of Australia. On the other hand, home language statistics do offer predictive value for future language maintenance/shift patterns.

In the next census I feel that we might learn more about language diversity if we asked people about the order in which their various languages have been acquired.

Ruth Hansford: How is the information obtained in the census used in policy-making?

Michael Clyne: It is used as the basis for languages-in-education policy, the distribution of radio transmission time, decisions on the location of adult migrant English classes, and the languages of certain public notices. There is one very real problem to do with the language statistics and the uses to which they are put, and that is the combining and collapsing of categories. For example, Chinese is given as one category, which is not at all helpful for those trying to provide any kind of support or service linked to the varieties spoken by the different Chinese groups in Australia. One wonders whether this sloppiness suggests that the information is not very highly regarded, since the necessary thinking has not gone into the statistical processing.

A second difficulty comes from the confidentiality necessary for any information deriving from the census. The statisticians refuse to break the data down into small units so that they can preserve respondents' anonymity and this means we cannot make the correlations that would be useful for educational services. So, all in all, the census has its limitations as a basis for policy making.

Lewis Glinert (SOAS, London): There is a further issue here. The notion 'community language' must not be taken as synonymous with 'community vernacular'. It is an unfortunate consequence of the modern linguistic emphasis on spoken language that the social role of written or primarily written languages has been neglected.

As Joshua Fishman has underlined in his work on the languages of the Great Traditions and Little Traditions[1] these languages frequently play a major role in modern societies, if typically a highly conflictual one. Our knowledge about the transmission, the perception and the functioning in diaspora of such languages as Polish within the Polish Catholic community, Sanskrit among Hindus, Punjabi among the Sikhs, Hebrew among Jews and Quranic Arabic among Muslims is very sketchy. What will happen to these languages as ties to the motherland weaken and maybe other kinds of ethnic ties, such as religious ones, take their place is a moot point. I am particularly interested in what happens when a language begins to lose any 'normal' communicative functions it may once have had and takes on mainly symbolic value. (In my own work, I have dubbed these varieties 'quasilects').

It will be a challenge to devise the right kinds of census questions to cope with such cases.

Li Wei (University of Newcastle): I agree that in some contexts, the written language is extremely important and will be maintained while the spoken is not or vice versa. Research and policy making ought to be aware of this.

Sue Wright (Aston University): The popular confusion between standardised written community language and community vernacular created educational problems in the UK during the 1980s. When local education authorities, such as Birmingham, introduced Urdu and Bengali into the curriculum, it was widely believed among teachers, education support staff and policy makers at the town hall that such measures would support and build on mother tongue through the acquisition of literacy. It took some time for the realisation that in many cases this was not so. For example, children from families of Pakistani origin in Birmingham enrolling on Urdu courses were, in most cases, acquiring a further foreign language. There is a large Mirpuri speaking population in the town — and, of course, this is a variety of Panjabi. Another example was the Sylheti speakers who were offered classes in Bengali, again a variety quite distinct from the language present in the community.

Of course this problem is not specific to community languages in the Australian or British context. It is the difficulty encountered every time a language is standardised by literature, the media, the educational system and state bureaucracies. In a previous issue of the journal, Charlotte Hoffmann[2]. described the plight of speakers of Galician who find that the newly standardised language of their Autonomy makes them a double minority — not mother tongue speakers of Castilian and users of a non-standard variety of Galician.

Manjula Datta (University of North London): It seems a cruel irony that some of these young people go through what can best be described as 'a double whammy' experience. First, they suffer the painful experience of losing their home language because the British education system doesn't include it. Then, when the language becomes available to them in the curriculum, it is not the language that they know. They may fail to meet the expectations of the host community — that they should be the mediators in trading relationships.

Stephen May (Bristol University): In my view, the question of multilingualism as an economic benefit is something of a two edged sword. For a start, it could be argued that Australia's multicultural/multilingual policy actually forms a part of the economic rationalist programme rather than opposing it. For example, Mary Kalantzis[3] has argued that the introduction of a multiculturalist policy in Australia was seen by some as a cost-cutting measure for government and a retreat from the principles of the welfare state via the contracting out of 'migrant services'.

Dennis Ager (Aston University): The principle that the state should not abdicate responsibilities towards sectors of society, by making them bear the costs and organisation of what may — for other groups — be borne by the state, is part of the French criticism of multiculturalism in Britain. The French hold that it leads to ghettoisation through differential treatment.[4]

John Rex (Warwick University): Some critics of multiculturalism have always argued that it promotes a kind of minorisation, which involves marking groups out for different — and inferior — treatment. Steve Vertovec argues that the very term ethnicity is only used in France to describe inferior people.

Manjula Datta: This feeling can be generated both within and outside the group. A proud Hindi-speaking father tried to tell me that his son had obtained an A grade in Hindi at GCSE level. His son interrupted, 'Dad, how can you boast about it? It's rubbish. It was a waste of time'. Maybe, the son felt that the course had not taken into account what he already knew, or that it had not taught him what he wanted to learn. But, in addition he was clearly not valuing the particular treatment the system had provided for him.

Kay Adamson: But this young man who feels his GCSE was a waste of time could be right if he had thought it was going to be about deepening his understanding of the language and culture. His interests are not going to be the same as someone whose need is general education and literacy in the language. To me this raises a major question about the basis of education. There are relatively few traditional educational systems, including those on the Indian sub-continent, where education/literacy is seen as being about the vernacular. The fact that we can refer to 'literary languages' means that a distinction is being made. Paulo Freire's work, I would have thought, has challenged that model. However, it seems to me that in this present debate over community languages the model itself is not being challenged.

Sue Wright: I think the distinction is understood by the groups concerned. Usually the desire to acquire literacy in the prestige variety comes from a set of rational decisions. In the case of someone deciding to become literate in Urdu rather than Mirpuri, we often find that individual choice stems from a desire for group cohesion and economic motivation. The decision may be prompted by a desire to acquire the language which permits contact throughout the whole Pakistani community in Britain and which allows access to the Pakistani diaspora media as well as providing most economic advantage in the case of a return to Pakistan.

Dennis Ager: We should stress this; economic utility is a prime motivation for both learner and provider. The philosophy of the market has been so strong in Britain in the last decade that it is only where groups can demonstrate clear economic benefits from the maintenance of their language that their case is taken seriously. This is translated into policy by the Category A and Category B languages in the National Curriculum. Category A consists of the languages of the EU and the most important trading nations in global terms; Category B includes the languages of the groups constituted by recent immigration.

Michael Clyne: But the designation of specific trade languages is problematic for the simple reason that we never know who our major trading partners will be in a decade, let alone in four. The argument should perhaps rather be that *any* biculturalism and bilingualism are of cognitive benefit as a preparation for a 'global person' of the 21st century.

Vanithamani Saravanan (Nanyang University, Singapore): Non-economically-motivated decisions may, however, in the end bring about positive economic results. For example, in Singapore the decision to promote Mandarin and Tamil was justified by the argument that they represented identities. Now, however, knowledge of these languages is contributing positively to the economy.

Stephen May: The argument for the economic value of multilingualism rests on the assumption that the minority languages present in the community have some instrumental value and/or economic collateral elsewhere. This is problematic on three counts. Firstly, it seems to me that economic arguments for language maintenance have tended to work against minority languages far more than for them. This is particularly evident with regard to the hegemonic influence of English, for example, and its role in minority language shift. Secondly, economic arguments for minority languages do not address the question of national minority languages that are not spoken elsewhere (e.g. Aboriginal languages, Maori, Welsh etc.). In fact, such arguments militate directly against the continuance of such languages. However, there are strong arguments for according these languages priority, given their historical associations with the nation-state and in relation to recognising the rights of those national minority groups who speak them. Thirdly, the multilingualism that Michael is describing seems to be limited to largely private domains and has, as such, little impact on the public culture of Australia which remains predominantly monolingual. In this respect, Australia is little different from most nation states which are predicated on the notion of a common civic language and culture. To what extent then are you overstating the case of a multilingual Australia? For such a case to be made, minority languages would need to be legitimated and institutionalised in the public domain and language use would have to impact on minority life chances, not just lifestyles.[5]

Michael Clyne: I agree to a certain extent. However, there are services provided in community languages across many public domains, such as official notices. And, would you regard state-run radio and TV stations as part of the private domain? The presence of community languages programmes in education and also the recognition of 43 languages as matriculation subjects means that language maintenance can affect people's life chances. Similarly there is a special languages allowance paid to members of the public service proficient in languages other than English. Perhaps one could say that monolingual English-speaking Australians are not disadvantaged structurally but under certain circumstances those highly proficient in English *and* another language can reap certain benefits.

In general, I agree with all that has been said about the dangers of the economic argument for languages, and yet there are ways in which it has benefited the position of languages other than English in schools and could be positive for migrants and their children. However, there is an exception to this and, as Stephen pointed out, indigenous languages are disadvantaged every time economic considerations come to the fore.

John Rex: I wonder if we could address the question of why the state should be asked to support multiculturalism. Many politicians as well as social scientists, particularly in France, assume that the purpose of the state should be to promote cultural homogeneity within which rational political action can be pursued.

Michael Clyne: Whether people maintain a language for one, two or three generations, giving them the opportunity to do so, in my opinion, makes a substantial contribution to social cohesion in a culturally diverse society in terms of fostering a feeling of belonging, furthering self-esteem and promoting good relations between generations.

Manjula Datta: Exactly. You can argue that multiculturalism benefits the majority as well as the minority. Multiculturalism encourages the development of skills such as identifying similarities and differences, comparing and contrasting, as well as bringing different perspectives to any learning issue — these are all valid academic skills which a policy of multiculturalism can develop in all children.

Sue Wright: We could extend John's question to multilingualism. Playing devil's advocate, I could put the point that multilingualism threatens the community of communication necessary for the interactions, the carrying on of tradition, the socialisation etc., etc. — all the language-based activities — which together help to build a nation.

Michael Clyne: I think that the need for a society to be homogeneous has been challenged by nations such as Australia. Supporting language maintenance where it is desired by the speakers and the provision of services in community languages doesn't mean undermining the significance of the national language, which is an important commodity from a socioeconomic point of view — particularly when it is English, the international language par excellence. The function of English as a lingua franca in the nation is not in question. We are talking about multiculturalism not ethnic separation.

Jenny Cheshire (QMW, London): Switzerland provides a good counter-example for people who argue that multilingualism is a handicap for a country, as Switzerland has the highest income per capita in Europe — and the lowest crime rate. Although it has four official languages, (German, French, Italian and Romansch), it still aims to construct a single national identity, albeit multilingual.

The national language policy rests on two principles. The first is the principle of individual choice, which enshrines in law the right of all Swiss citizens to use whichever of the official languages they prefer. The second is the principle of territoriality, which gives every Swiss canton the right to decide on the language that will be the official one within that canton. There are four bilingual cantons, but the rest are monolingual. These two principles place a burden on the education system, because for the Swiss to be able to exercise the principle of individual choice when they communicate, school children have to learn some of the other Swiss languages. The national policy aims to achieve this through the Partner language model, whereby schoolchildren learn as their second language the language of their neighbouring canton. But the model doesn't work too well in practice. This is partly because the German-speaking part of Switzerland is an example of 'leaky diglossia', with the German speakers nowadays using their dialects increasingly often in domains where standard (High) German used to be the norm. This means that the other language groups now have little motivation for learning German at school, since they cannot use it to understand the German-speaking Swiss, nor can they reinforce their second language learning by listening to radio or television. Moreover, the younger age groups often prefer to use English, the language of international youth culture, rather than the language of their neighbouring canton. So young people accept their multilingual national identity, but multilingualism for them can often be symbolic rather than a reality.

Helen Kelly-Holmes (Aston University): I wonder if we could clarify what we actually mean by multiculturalism as intended by the policy in Australia. Is it a desire to expose the majority of children (from a variety of cultural backgrounds) to the cultures and languages of their fellow citizens or is it simply a wish to preserve these cultures for the particular groups that claim them.

Michael Clyne: I think it has probably attempted to achieve both. Perhaps I should also say that multiculturalism means many things to different people and is not a well-defined policy.

Helen Kelly-Holmes: It is clear from your paper that the composite classroom — with background and non-background speakers — was actually a success for multiculturalism and pluralism, in that non-background speakers wanted to learn the languages of immigrant groups. It seems a pity that this success should now be seen in terms of problems and unfairness.

Dennis Smith (Aston University): Would you say that your findings present an interesting commentary upon Bourdieu's treatment of 'cultural capital'? He argues that in the French case the latent benefits derived from an upper middle class family background such as going to the opera are not penalised — nor would it be conceivable that they should be. They are not even explicitly recognised. But when the children of recent immigrants have an advantage in certain language examinations, the Australian system comes down on them like a ton of bricks.

Michael Clyne: Yes and isn't it quite paradoxical? Once minorities are recognised as possessing important cultural capital, some people think it has to be taken away from them!

Stephen Barbour (Middlesex University): From my work in the European context, I have come to expect language maintenance to be supported most strongly by intellectual elites. They tend to see language as a core value, to which they are prepared to allocate resources — time, money, effort. Do you have similar findings in the Australian context?

Michael Clyne: Smolicz found in studies carried out in the University of Adelaide that for some cultural groups, languages represent a core value. Such languages tend to be maintained well. I'm not sure that we have specific correlations between intellectual elites and maintenance. In any case, there is a mismatch between what people say they wish to do with regard to language maintenance and what they actually do.

Stephen Barbour: Different language groups seem to allocate strikingly different levels of importance to language as a marker of ethnic or national identity. In areas with English-speaking majorities it seems to have relatively little importance. One can, for example, have a clear Irish identity without fluency in the Irish language. In some other areas language seems to be *the* decisive factor in people's identity.

Sue Wright: The phenomenon of hyphenated identities in the US (e.g. Irish-American, Italian-American) seems to lend itself to identity patterns which do not include language. For such groups, the original language becomes superfluous for communication, since all members of the group, after the first generation, speak American English, while the "first" element of the identity has largely become a matter of memory, tradition and limited cultural practices, which seems to be transmitted quite well without detailed knowledge of the original language.

Michael Clyne: In the first generation, language maintenance is clearly a matter of communicative necessity, whereas in the second and later generations, it is due to an ideological commitment towards bilingualism.

Kay Adamson (Sunderland University): Are people who are multi/bilingual in their country of origin more likely to continue to be multilingual in the Australian context compared to immigrants who come from monolingual countries? And I'm not referring here just to monolingual English speakers but also to those who make the switch from monolingualism in another language to monolingualism in English. I ask the question because there has been some work done by Christopher Bagley[6] on maths aptitude of immigrants in Canada, which showed that new immigrants from maths literate societies reflected the practice of their country of origin for an initial period but then lost this advantage over time to come into line with the standard in their new country. In other words they lost skills. Does the monolingualism of the new country influence multilingual immigrants in a similar way? Do the group's linguistic skills come to mirror those of the majority.

Michael Clyne: There is evidence that those with pre-immigration language maintenance experience continue to maintain their community language more or longer than those from monolingual environments. Among examples are ethnic Germans from Eastern Europe and the Middle East, Latvians, and Russians from China.

Kay Adamson: Can language maintenance be seen to be maintaining a certain male power within some communities? This could mean that there may be complex and differential reasons for women and men to retain the mother tongue.

Sue Wright: Work that we did in Birmingham in the late 1980s revealed a correlation between commitment to language maintenance and gender. Young males were much more likely to attend classes and take other measures to maintain their mother tongues than young women. The reasons that young women gave for not taking part in this maintenance were varied, but one interesting and contentious reason given was that language competence made it easier for them to be considered for arranged marriages with boys from the family's country of origin. While they were not against arranged marriages as such, they did not want to marry people not born, like them, in the UK.

The other factor which makes it more likely that men will conserve the language is the role of the mosque in the process. Most of our Muslim subjects were acquiring literacy in mosque classes, which were not available to young women.

Michael Clyne: Other statistics suggest that women generally maintain community languages more than men, but the differential gradually decreases inter-generationally. Recent work by Anne Pauwels indicates that the reasons for language maintenance are also gender-dependent.

Deirdre Martin (Birmingham University): Can I ask you for the basis of your prediction that the number of speakers of Spanish will increase, that Chinese speakers will outnumber Greek and that Vietnamese will replace German as the fifth largest community language? Is it because of new immigration or a rise in the birth rate in these communities? Or is it because these speakers now feel more confident about admitting that they have more than English in their repertoire. Public attitudes towards plurilingualism and the maintenance of linguistic variety in Australia are now much more positive.

Michael Clyne: In the case of Chinese and Vietnamese it is a combination of new immigration and the birth of second generation speakers. Among Spanish speakers the reasons are these, combined with an increasing tendency towards inter-generational language maintenance among Latin-American Australians. At the same time, some of the first generation speakers of older established community languages such as German are dying.

Manjula Datta: In the UK there has been no coherent governmental policy regarding multilingualism. Most initiatives in the 1980s originated in the more enlightened local authorities but were never adopted wholesale. With the introduction of the National Curriculum, community language teaching was eclipsed by foreign language teaching. Government directives demanded that the Section 11 funding that had been used for mother tongue teaching be used for ESOL only. It is alarming to hear schools openly declaring themselves 'English-only' schools, and in most school language policies it is clear that 'valuing home languages' now has only the status of a paper-tiger! A great number of teachers still do not have any knowledge about what languages their pupils speak. The effective learning of English is defeated by monolingual policy and practice. In Britain we seem to have returned to the old days — the situation that you describe in the early part of your paper.

Michael Clyne: I am sorry to hear this. Perhaps the time has come for those favouring more pluralist policies in different countries to start talking to each other about what we most want to defend. One of the important tasks is to ensure that core curricula where they are introduced are not monocultural or monolingual. In Australia, there is now a danger that paranoia created by politicians about English literacy standards could damage the core position recently won for languages other than English on primary and secondary curricula under the pretext of the school time table being too overcrowded. In the British case, I fear that European integration has meant not only pluralist policies which are to be welcomed but also the reversal of hard-won inclusion, which is not.

Notes

1. Fishman, J. (1972) *Language and Nationalism: Two Integrative Essays.* Rowley, Mass: Newbury House.
2. Hoffmann, C. (1995) Twenty years of language planning in contemporary Spain. In S. Wright (ed.) *Monolingualism and Bilingualism Lessons from Canada and Spain.* Clevedon: Multilingual Matters.
3. Kalantzis, M. and Cope, B. (1998) Pedagogy after Pluralism: How multicultural education can reconstitute the mainstream. In S. May (ed.) *Critical Multiculturalism: Rethinking Multicultural and Antiracist Education.* London: Falmer Press.
4. Dennis Smith develops these points in his written reply.
5. Stephen May develops these points in his written reply.
6. Bagley, C. (1989) Education for all: A Canadian dimension. In G. Verma (ed.) *Education for All — A Landmark in Pluralism.* London: Falmer Press.

The Misery and the Splendour of Multiculturalism: A Response to Michael Clyne

John E. Joseph
Department of Applied Linguistics, The University of Edinburgh, 14 Buccleuch Place, Edinburgh EH8 9LN

Michael Clyne's pride in today's very multilingual and multicultural Australia is well founded. Attempts by foreign news media to portray a ground swell of racist sentiment there are not terribly convincing.[1] Clyne's work has undoubtedly contributed to the positive situation in Australia, by improving scholarly understanding of Australian multilingualism and, even more importantly, influencing educational policy.

There is however a particular problem with *multiculturalism*, which is more or less equated with multilingualism in Professor Clyne's article. For a concept that originated as such a splendid vision, it has endured a miserable fate (hence the allusion in my title to Ortega y Gasset's essay on translation). The term has become such a lightning rod that one fears it might work against its proponents' admirable aims. It is clear that Clyne is fully aware of the dangers I am referring to, but has chosen the path of idealism and optimism, a hard choice to fault. And after all, to give up a worthy concept just because it has come under attack would be craven. So two cheers for Clyne, one for optimism and the other for sticking to his guns.

But hold the third cheer until after a few words from your devoted worrywart, who thinks that, all the same, talking through the hostility we take on for ourselves in some quarters by casting our lot with multiculturalism is the best preparation for fighting back. (Stubborn, optimistic idealists like Clyne always need to have other people do this worrying for them, publicly at least.) It is, by the way, not just the foes of multiculturalism we have to worry about. Some of its more fervent champions give no less cause for alarm.

As I pointed out during the debate following Clyne's paper, for many people multiculturalism is synonymous with *cultural relativism*. The very mention of multiculturalism is taken to imply that the artistic masterpieces of the Italian Renaissance are on a par with Inuit scrimshaw or black velvet paintings of Elvis. In other words, the products of Western culture which the culture itself considers to be its masterpieces must be evaluated as no better than what any other culture regards as its own works of art (the scrimshaw example). Or in a more extreme form, no cultural product can be justifiably considered as superior to any other, without engaging in a form of power which is as artificial and illegitimate as it is repressive (the black velvet Elvis example). This latter is the really problematic interpretation. Although it must be admitted that many vocal proponents of multiculturalism do hold to it, they are nowhere near so numerous as the concept's foes imagine.

Linking multilingualism with multiculturalism seems like a natural extension of the link between language and culture, on which language professionals, linguists and language teachers alike, regularly fall back when justifying our work to research support agencies and institutional administrators and advertising it to potential students. The language-culture link raises problems of its own, including why it is that all speakers of the same language do not perceive things in the same way, to the point that they do not even agree about the meanings of words in their language (as recognised by no less canonical a Western author than Locke 1690), or how it is possible for a single language such as English to support the number of widely differing cultures it does.[2]

For present purposes what matters is that multiculturalism does not require multilingualism. Edwards (1985), focusing on the case of Ireland, has demonstrated empirically that culture can be maintained indefinitely beyond the loss of language. Logically too it must be possible for a monolingual to be multicultural, unless one is prepared to hold that no one can know a culture without speaking its language. That would make multiculturalism an unreachable goal, since no one can possibly learn the languages of all the cultures which multiculturalists would have us engage with. Multiculturalism would be reduced to absurdity.

To assert that one can only *really* know a culture whose language one has studied in depth is not multiculturalism but its direct opposite: it is the traditional view of Western scholarship. This traditional view is not hostile to the study of cultures other than its own or even of the 'vernacular' products of culture. It maintains however that education should consist of first mastering the high points of Western culture before pursuing the rest. This guarantees that the foreign and the vernacular will be fitted into the uniform framework defined by the Western classics. Multiculturalism, on the other hand, wants to disestablish the initial uniformity, or at least to expand it so that it is no longer centred upon one type of product from one particular culture. The debate, in other words, is about whether cultural multiplicity should enter early and be part of general education or enter late and be reserved for people who, having already completed their basic training, can afford to dabble or specialise in the 'exotic'.

To my knowledge no one has ever argued that Western education should entirely exclude non-Western or vernacular cultures. Yet the more resolute foes of multiculturalism react as though a broadening of the cultural base of general education were tantamount to undermining everything Western education has been about for 2500 years. This runs so directly contrary to fact as to appear irrational. Perhaps it can be ascribed, like racism, to a psychological defence against the desire we experience for what is different and exotic, in which excitement and horror become fused.[3] It would be tempting to dismiss reactions against multiculturalism in this way were it not for those overzealous proponents who think that we *really should* be undermining everything Western education has been about for 2500 years, on the grounds that this may release and redeem us from our history as a culture oppressive to outsiders and to most of its own members.

The multiculturalism I believe in, which I expect is also the one Michael Clyne believes in, is instead a tempered version of the scrimshaw interpretation, and includes these beliefs:

- the products of any culture are intrinsically of interest, and some potentially of great interest, to people from outside that culture;
- the products of any culture can be evaluated as better or worse, great or awful, in terms of that culture's own system of values, which other cultures should try to take into account (but need not, and certainly will not always) when making their own evaluations;
- the products of a culture are not entirely separable from the history of the people who produced them, yet deep and subtle understanding of that history will rarely justify outright rejection of the products on the grounds that their producers or the process of their production were cartoon-character evil;
- appreciation of the best products of other cultures should not replace or compete with appreciation of the best of one's own culture, but should supplement and enhance it.

This last belief is the crux. The foes of multiculturalism often assume that behind it is a kind of mental decadence that makes people too lazy to bother with the intricacies of 'high' culture. My multiculturalism appreciates that all cultures have their own intricacy, and because it insists on an appreciation of both Western and non-Western cultures, it demands a huge investment of human effort. From this point of view, it is the opponents of multiculturalism who are mentally lazy.

On the other hand, it has to be acknowledged that the weakest point of my interpretation of multiculturalism is that it demands more time and effort than a lot of people, including full-time students, are able to give once the daily exigencies of modern life have been met. I admit that it is an idealistic interpretation, though that is not the same as calling it an unrealistic one. As educators it is up to us to turn ideals into reality, and therein lie the misery and the splendour of education.

Opening a gallery of exotic or postmodern art is likely to be only mildly scandalous, unless one sins by being too traditionalist.[4] But then, no one would be so foolhardy as to bulldoze a gallery of Western art to build a non-Western one. Yet introducing anything non-Western or non-mainstream into the school curriculum always means replacing something Western and mainstream. That is where the trouble arises. If I were Minister for Multiculturalism I would argue for extending the school day or year or preferably both so that much could be added and nothing lost. I would, of course, enjoy a term of office of less than 48 hours from the moment I made this proposal public, forced out by general outcry, the loudest cries of all coming no doubt from the teachers' unions.

It is because school hours are unlikely to expand to the extent necessary to have multiculturalism without shallowness — splendid rather than miserable multiculturalism — that language professionals run a risk in putting ourselves forward as educational multiculturalists. Again, I am not saying we should abandon the goal of multiculturalism, just that we should do what we can to lessen the risk relative to the potential reward. In this respect we would do well to incorporate into our advocacy of language study some avowedly traditionalist considerations, starting with the fact that *the Western educational tradition has throughout its entire history been heavily language-focused*, with the basis for all further education being grammar and rhetoric, nearly always based on the study of a language other than the mother tongue, including the classical languages.

The single most dramatic change in this tradition in the last hundred years has been the crumbling of the classical languages and their literatures as the core of Western education. The idea that their place could fall to the study of certain modern Western languages with their own great literatures is what led to the rise of the modern language professions as we know them. But then this belief retreated with the spread of two other trendy views which seemed to enjoy the backing of the newer American linguistics: first that whatever knowledge stood to be gained from the study of language could best be accessed by reflection on one's mother tongue, and secondly that traditional grammar was not a useful tool for either the understanding of language structure or the learning of foreign languages. Unfortunately, the mastery of traditional grammar was also one of the primary rationales offered for the study of foreign languages. If grammar has no usefulness as a means, what value could it possibly have as an end in itself to be pursued through language study?

These developments are directly responsible for the monolingualisation of education in recent decades. Admittedly they may have been helped along by the signals they seemed to send about cultural homogeneity and national coherence to governments of countries like Australia, the US and Canada, whose populations had always been diverse and were becoming increasingly so. Now that same diversity appears to present an opportunity for reviving support for language study and education based on the desirability for multiculturalism.

However, for those opposed to multiculturalism to be encouraged by us language professionals to equate multilingual education with antitraditionalism and cultural relativism is hugely ironic and counterproductive. Multilingual education is the core of the Western educational tradition, where for some 2000 years it was the anchor for Western cultural *absolutism*, though the experience of much of the 20th century showed that it need not be so. The point is that *multilingual education transcends the dichotomy between Western traditionalism and multiculturalism*, and its transcendence risks being missed if it is tied too closely and exclusively to the multiculturalist agenda.[5] The language-culture link has been deployed by language professionals, sometimes in spurious ways, as the traditional role of language study in education has declined. There are also non-spurious ways of deploying it, and these should be pursued — but no less as paths to the deep knowledge of cultures which traditionalism demands than to the broader knowledge advocated by multiculturalism. Moreover, the link should be invoked not to replace but to supplement independent arguments for why, for its own sake, we should study how people talk, ourselves and others.

Finally, a comment about the ultimate misery of multiculturalism for many of us who aspire to its splendour: the disdain its most fervent proponents have shown for freedom of speech. Even Clyne, the soul of reasonableness, can barely contain his contempt for those who make racist remarks then cry 'freedom of speech' when called to account for them. Like multilingual education, freedom of speech transcends the dichotomy of multiculturalism and Western traditionalism — and so does racism. One of the most positive developments to have occurred in Western societies in the last quarter century has been the virtual elimination (or at least the complete marginalisation) of overt racism from acceptable public discourse, not through legislation, but through a surprisingly rapid evolution of the parameters of civilised thought and behaviour. Racist speech still occurs. It is morally reprehensible and inflicts damage on individuals and society at large. Speech which is damaging to individuals, such as libel, or to society, such as subversion, are not protected in common law jurisdictions. Political speech is protected. In the case of libel, the protection of political content is held to outweigh damage to the individual in the US if the individual is a public figure, though not in the UK and most other common law countries.

Racist 'hate speech' is somewhat comparable to libel of a public figure in that it can combine political opinion with personal damage which is not strictly personal, being directed at the race rather than the individual who is the immediate target, just as the libel may be directed at the individual as holder of an office or position rather than as a person. Some regulations against hate speech have included an assertion that damage inflicted to an entire race by words is *worse* than damage to the individual person. The problem is that it is very difficult to draw the line at which words spoken against an entire group of people ceases to be political, whether in the case of racism or of subversion. If political speech is not protected — and not just the political speech the majority believe in, but that which they find reprehensible — the very cornerstone of democracy and liberal society is destroyed, and with them goes any hope for the freedom of minority groups and individuals. Multiculturalists who see it as in their interest to undermine the cause of free speech are being short-sighted. Free speech is, to a large extent, what multiculturalism is itself about — the rights of voices from outside the Western mainstream to be heard.

True multiculturalists should not have the instincts to silence others. But every time freedom of speech is belittled in the name of multiculturalism, its opponents' worst fears appear to be confirmed — that the multiculturalist agenda inevitably means the loss of all that is best in Western culture, including its liberal democratic values. Multiculturalism need not and must not mean that. Multilingualism and language education should steer miles clear of it.

However much one may be committed to the best of what multiculturalism can be about, it is a minefield. By keeping one foot out of it, we double our chances of getting the agenda of multilingual education through intact. Ultimately the language professions will be best served by separating multilingualism from multiculturalism as distinct battles. They are not in fact about the same thing. Both battles deserve to be fought and won. One of them is a particularly uphill struggle made all the more so by well-intentioned enemies within.

Notes

1. It may be that anywhere in the world racial intolerance is just an economic recession away from bubbling to the surface. Yet one would be hard put to find another country with so diverse a population that has gone as far as Australia has in reconciling the divides between aboriginals and immigrants on the one hand, and various waves of immigrants on the other. This is not what other countries want to hear which hold themselves up as models of racial tolerance (sometimes by force majeure, as in Singapore or the pre-breakup USSR; or simply ludicrously, as in the case of France) or console themselves that their racial tensions are inevitable and in any case are no worse than anyone else's (the US and Britain being prime examples).

2. An interesting moment occurred in the debate following Clyne's paper when Sue Wright quite rightly noted a Sapirian-Whorfian thread running through his arguments, which Clyne quite rightly tried to distance himself from by asserting that 'culture is dynamic'. Joseph (1996) discusses the extent to which the 'Sapir-Whorf hypothesis' was formulated as propaganda for linguistics, precisely through asserting a strong language-culture link that could only be understood by studying the structures of non-Western languages.
3. Young (1994) makes a strong case for interpreting racist discourse in this way.
4. Although I have begun with examples from art, that is an area of Western culture which has in fact been very multicultural for a long time. Western religions too have warmed surprisingly in recent decades to the notion of their continuity with non-Western traditions. The most resistant areas are science and especially philosophy. Those who argue that the logic which underlies Western philosophy and science should not be privileged over other ways of reasoning still constitute an avant garde, and it is they, rather than their artistic counterparts, who are the spectres most feared by opponents of multiculturalism.
5. I expect this is a point with which Michael Clyne will agree; indeed he may feel that it is too obvious to need stating. But a number of the comments made in the discussion period were aimed in this direction, and the point is too important to worry about overemphasising it.

References

Edwards, J. (1985) *Language, Society and Identity*. Oxford and New York: Basil Blackwell, in association with André Deutsch.

Joseph, J.E. (1996) The immediate sources of the 'Sapir-Whorf Hypothesis'. *Historiographia Linguistica* 23, 365–404.

Locke, J. (1690) *An Essay Concerning Humane Understanding*. London: Thomas Basset.

Ortega y Gasset, J. (1937) La miseria y el esplendor de la traducción, *La Nación* (Buenos Aires), May–June 1937. (English version, 'The misery and the splendor of translation' translated by Elizabeth Gamble Miller. In R. Schulte and J. Biguenet (eds) (1992) *Theories of Translation: An Anthology of Essays from Dryden to Derrida*. Chicago and London: University of Chicago Press).

Young, Robert C. (1994) *Colonial Desire*. London and New York: Routledge.

Michael Clyne comments:

I agree that multilingualism should not be equated with multiculturalism. However, there is an important link. I do believe that the value of multilingualism in Australia needs to be justified socially (integratively) and/or economically (instrumentally) and not through Western cultural traditions because of the anti-intellectualism and utilitarianism that has pervaded Australian thinking.

Cultural Democracy and Cultural Capital — Some Reflections on the Australian Case: A Response to Michael Clyne

Dennis Smith
Aston Business School, South Wing (10), Aston University, Aston Triangle,
Birmingham B4 7ET

In his paper entitled 'Managing language diversity and second language programmes in Australia' (Clyne, 1997), Michael Clyne explores the way state language-in-education practices have been affected by the disintegration of national languages policy, the rise of 'anti-social attitudes' and growing emphasis on the desirability of actively responding to market pressures. In fact, the paper works at two levels simultaneously. At one level, it is concerned with the details of language maintenance and shift in respect of specific language groups and, in this context, reports on two research projects conducted by the Language and Society Centre at Monash. However, at another level, an argument is presented about the broader socio-economic and political context. Clyne suggests that three tensions lie at the heart of the current debate. These are: firstly, between the special interests of a wide variety of language groups and the universalistic standards imposed by the market criteria favoured by economic neo-liberals; secondly, between, on the one hand, the interests of a greatly expanded educational sector promoted by an articulate lobby of experts and, on the other hand, the standards and concerns of 'a basically utilitarian and anti-intellectual society'; and thirdly, between Australia's national self-image as a classless and egalitarian society providing opportunity for all, and the resentment stirred up among 'old' Australians at the educational advantage possessed by 'new' Australians, often from poor socio-economic circumstances, on account of their special language skills.

The present situation, as Clyne describes it, is regarded as unsatisfactory by two constituencies. One of these consists of the supporters of the federal Liberal-National Party coalition who hanker after the 1950s when 'white' Australia insisted on instant assimilation of immigrants to the 'Anglo-Saxon' culture dominant at that time. This culture is still strongly valued among the older generation, especially in the rural communities of Western Australia and Queensland. The other constituency adheres to values which were dominant during the 1970s. In that period, cultural diversity, multiple identity and social justice became central concerns of government. Australians were encouraged to think of themselves as belonging to a richly multicultural nation which should cultivate its links with the rest of the Asia-Pacific region. The growth points of this new Australia were urban rather than rural, among the young rather than the old, and in Melbourne (Victoria) and, especially, Sydney (New South Wales) rather than Perth (Western Australia) or Brisbane (Queensland). Like many language-policy professionals, Clyne clearly prefers the latter set of values although his evidence effectively undermines the idea that Australia is 'some kind of multicultural utopia'.

Clyne shows that during the late 1990s there is intense competition between these two interests. Contributors to the debate over language policy typically draw upon one set of values to attack the other. For example, the 'old' values of the 1950s are attacked as 'racist' by adherents of the 'new' values of the 1970s. In return, members of the 'Anglo-Saxon' tendency complain about the dogmas of 'political correctness' which have grown up since the 1970s. However, this two-way competition has been complicated by the emergence of a third force in the policy arena. This is the demand for policies based on the Friedmanite or Thatcherite strategy of economic neo-liberalism (or 'rationalism' as Clyne prefers to call it). This approach sees languages as potential resources that can be mobilised to exploit market opportunities. More specifically, the population's ability to speak and understand a wide variety of languages should be encouraged insofar as this increases the potential effectiveness of contacts with potential trade partners; in other words, insofar as it helps to improve the capacity of the Australian economy to generate profits.

In fact, economic rationalism was already making its weight felt by the 1980s. By the latter half of that decade the 'Community Language Multiculturalists' were losing ground to the 'Anglo-Asianists', to borrow the terms used by Joseph LoBianco (Lo Bianco, 1987). The latter were, in Clyne's parlance, 'economic rationalists'. They saw Chinese and Japanese as 'key' or 'front-line' languages, clearly relevant to Australia's national interest. Those languages should be encouraged since they would make a strong contribution to economic development in Australia. Advocates of other minority languages should, it was argued, make out a similar economic case if they were to be taken seriously. As far as the Anglo-Asianists were concerned, many of the Community Language Multi-culturalists failed to make this case. They were obsessed with 'useless' languages and sectarian causes (Lo Bianco, 1987: 72).

As a historical sociologist with an interest in nation-building and the development of capitalist democracy, I was particularly struck by three aspects of Clyne's paper: firstly, the links he points to between global capitalism, geopolitics, nation-state development, migration and language policy; secondly, the value of his paper as a 'report from the front line' on the multiple overlapping dilemmas with respect to goals and values faced by the interests groups involved in language policy; and, thirdly, the implications of language policy issues for our theoretical understanding of ethnicity, social stratification and capitalist democracy. These will be considered in turn.

At least three sets of power relationships mould a nation's language policy. These are the structure of international relations, both political and economic, the leverage within these global structures exercised by the nation's politicians and business interests, and the balance of influence between competing language communities within the nation. The interplay between these three sets is very complex and cannot be explored in detail here. However, some broad issues may be identified by taking two contrasting cases, the United States and Belgium, both multi-lingual and multi-cultural societies. As the United States came to dominate the global economic and diplomatic arena during the 1940s and 1950s, this process confirmed the supremacy of the English language as the primary medium of international trade and commerce. During the century before the United States achieved this hegemonic position, the global reach of the British Empire had already established English as the language of international influence. Immigrants to America from non-English speaking societies had considerable incentive to learn English, the language of the Declaration of Independence and the American Constitution, documents which appeared to guarantee equal rights and opportunities to individuals irrespective of their cultural backgrounds. English was the language of the leading American business and political establishments, the lingua franca of international communication, and, not least, the language in which the ideals of democracy were expressed. Learning English was a central act in acquiring citizenship and becoming American. At the same time, American culture made room for a wide range of hyphenated identities, Italian-American, Polish-American and so on. In the early stages of an immigrant community's career, these hyphenated identities could be the basis for political organisation in the inner city. As subsequent generations moved out to the suburbs and made their way through the education system and into the professions and corporate structures, families were able to put on or discard these hyphenated identities at will, without necessarily maintaining the old familiarity with the language of their country of origin outside the United States.[1]

Since the 1970s there has been a strong revival of ethnic feeling within the United States. In particular, the rapid growth of the Latino population in many cities and states has led to a demand that the Spanish language be given greatly increased recognition. I would argue that this movement is strongly, although certainly not entirely, related to the considerable setback in prestige suffered by the Washington political establishment during and after the Vietnam War. This defeat was a dramatic illustration of a long-term decline in the international position of the United States, especially in relation to the leading Asian societies. This decline certainly does not mean that the English language will cease to be a highly convenient medium for international business. However, it does mean that well-organised and determined language pressure groups within the United States can assert themselves more effectively against an Anglicised federal political establishment which has suffered highly visible defeats at the hands of non-English speaking forces in the international arena with a consequent weakening of authority in all areas.

Imagine a possible future United States that has been pushed out of Asia, that has become inward-looking, that is increasingly anxious about a rapidly growing Latin America just to the south. Imagine an increasingly powerful and assertive Latino interest within the United States, one that gains permanent control of key cities and states, one that, perhaps by this time, has seen Quebec successfully achieve a high degree of independence within Canada. Is it totally unthinkable that the United States might experience political devolution into 'Anglo-Saxon' and 'Latino' regions, perhaps with a confederation of Spanish-speaking states emerging alongside a similar confederation of English-speaking states, both under the umbrella of the federal government in Washington (or elsewhere)? Looking even further ahead, might not the American continent, north and south, find considerable advantage in establishing a strong single market, perhaps with a common currency? Would not such an arrangement give strength to devolutionary pressures within all the American nation-states, as well as raising questions about the relative priority of English, Spanish and, indeed, Portuguese within the pan-American arena?

These speculations obviously beg several questions but they establish a key link with the Belgian case. Belgium shared in the global power enjoyed by Western Europe until the mid-twentieth century. French and Dutch, the languages of the Walloon and Flemish parts of the Belgian population, are both 'imperialistic' tongues, languages spoken by conquerors. In this respect they resemble English and Spanish, the equivalent languages in the American case imagined above. During World War II Belgium's political establishment suffered cruelty and humiliation at the hands of the Nazi regime of a far worse kind than any indignities suffered by Washington in the 1960s and 1970s. The Belgian economy and Belgian state have had to adapt to global conditions over which they have relatively little influence and obey rules made by others. One way they adapted after the war was by taking a strong lead in the movement for European integration. The biggest losers in all these changes have been members of the French-speaking minority who have, historically, had the upper hand within Belgium's political and business establishments. Despite continuing efforts to strengthen the influence of French as a rival to English in the European and world arenas, the Walloon interest within Belgium has suffered a considerable loss of prestige during the past half century. Since the war, the desire of the Flemish majority for greater recognition and rights has become increasingly difficult to resist. Finally, in 1994, Belgium became a federal state with three unilingual areas (Dutch, French, German) and the bilingual area of metropolitan Brussels.[2] It seems likely that this outcome was made easier to bring about by the strengthening of supra-state institutions at the European level. Although there is a parallel between present-day Belgium and one possible future for the United States, the continuing dominance of English within the United States for the forseeable future means that important differences exist between the two societies in respect of how ethnicity and language are handled, socially and politically. As has been argued, Americans who wish to preserve and cultivate a distinct ethnic identity (e.g. Italian, Japanese, Mexican) while taking advantage of their citizenship rights (as voters, students, welfare beneficiaries and so on) find themselves in a 'hyphenated' situation. This option does not exist in Belgium. There are no hyphenated Belgians, just a divided Belgium.[3]

This brief comparison between Belgium and the United States has raised many more issues than can be properly pursued here. It is simply intended to establish three points: first, it is impossible to divorce the discussion of language from a consideration of power; second, power is an attribute of complex relationships between groups within and between societies; and third, the task of understanding the part played by language is inseparable from the task of teasing out the dynamics of change over time within these complex power relationships. This perspective may now be applied to the Australian case more directly.

For a long time, the close economic, political and cultural links Australia maintained with Britain ensured the domination of English language and culture while also enabling Australians to feel separate from and superior to their Pacific neighbours. Unlike the United States, however, Australian English did not enshrine any great explicit codification of universal citizenship rights. Instead, it was a communication medium for an Anglo-Saxon culture that was often perceived from the outside as being inward-looking and intolerant of other languages, nations and cultures. Since the 1960s, the global balance of power has shifted substantially away from the Atlantic and towards the Pacific. American capitalism has been forced to give ground before the 'tiger economies' of Southeast Asia. In the wake of this change, Australia's situation is, in some respects, like Belgium, in others like the United States. Like the United States, Australia has received successive waves of non English-speaking immigrants into a society whose dominant establishments are English-speaking. Like Belgium in Europe, Australia has become a deeply involved but secondary participant in the thriving capitalist arena of Southeast Asia whose leading players are Japan and China.

The implications of this international situation for relations between ethnic groups within Australia are complex. On the one hand, the enormous significance of the Pacific market has improved the power situation of 'new' Australians who speak the languages of that area: Chinese, Japanese and so on. On the other hand, the secondary status of the Australian economy and the Australian state within this larger arena means that the growing influence of the new Australians produces nervousness among adherents of 'old' Australia, the Australia of the 1950s. Their attitudes were shaped by a previous era of British, and subsequently American, global domination. The new situation of the 1990s produces a series of understandable anxieties. For example, how much regard to the interests and sensitivities of 'old' Australians will be shown by 'new' Australians who retain strong family links to the Asian societies from which they originated? How far can Australia's business people and politicians depend upon English remaining the lingua franca of Southeast Asian international trade, as it is elsewhere in the world? Assuming that economic benefits flow from knowing the languages of the Pacific region, that such skills do indeed bring added value, how much effort should be put into encouraging native English speakers to acquire them? To what extent should reliance be placed on the existing linguistic resources represented by the inherited competences of Asian-Australians? These issues arouse considerable passion. For example, Community Language Multiculturalists accused Anglo-Asianists 'of not "trusting" Asian-Australians who, by the community language thrust, would "inevitably" be more proficient speakers of the so-called "key" languages than would Anglo-Australians' (Lo Bianco, 1987: 72).

A more general point is that neither the strength and content of the ethnic identity of an individual or a group are fixed. Particular aspects of ethnic identity may be emphasised or played down according to circumstances. It is striking, for example, that during and after the First World War, German-Americans were generally not keen to draw attention to their particular European roots (Holli, 1981). Similarly, Germans with Jewish backgrounds hid the fact, where possible, during the 1930s. Among those who survived the Holocaust by fleeing from Germany in the early 1930s, some (such as Hannah Arendt) rejected their German identity and emphasised their Jewishness while others, such as Norbert Elias retained a strong sense of being German.[4] In this context it is worth asking what part 'Anglo-Saxon' intolerance (or racism) plays in encouraging Australian ethnic minorities to seek collective solidarity by promoting their own cultures? Would a lessening of white bigotry have the paradoxical effect of reducing the political appeal and effectiveness of pressure-groups promoting minority languages, in the long run at least? Is there is a 'natural' alliance between socio-linguists and language-policy professionals on the one hand and, on the other, members of language groups who feel oppressed or neglected? All these groups have a heightened sensitivity to the active role of language in society whereas members of the dominant group, whose own language is the primary medium of communication, typically remain blind to this role.

A second issue latent in Clyne's paper is the meaning of 'cultural democracy', a term given widespread currency following the publication in 1984 of the report produced by the task force investigating multiculturalism and education (Smolicz *et al.*, 1984). The term 'cultural democracy' is not a straightforward one, a fact which produces both costs and benefits. On the one hand, language policy is, perhaps inevitably, located in a highly politicised area. A certain amount of strategic ambiguity in terminology may be useful for maximising support from as broad a coalition of interests as possible in the scramble for resources. On the other hand, however, it may be argued that the term 'cultural democracy' has at least two meanings which are potentially opposed to each other in some respects. The term may mean a 'democracy of cultures', in other words, a system of resource distribution which ensures that money, opportunities for advancement, and the enjoyment of status and respect are shared fairly, that is, in such a way that no particular group of minority cultures and languages is systematically treated as being in all or most respects 'worse' or 'better' than all the others. A democracy of cultures is achieved when representatives of all cultures within a polity have an equal 'place at the table', an equal right or, better still, an equal capacity to bid : *r* or, better still, obtain, the rewards generated by the society. The United Nations provides one international model, albeit an imperfect one, for a democracy of cultures.

An alternative meaning of 'cultural democracy' is 'democratic culture', or, perhaps, 'culture for democracy'. In this case, the term signifies the universal acceptance within a society of values and social practices which give positive support to communication, cooperation and understanding among all members of the society. A democratic culture takes as its basic 'unit' the individual rather than the language community as a whole. Advocates of such a culture would oppose any effort by religious leaders, cultural traditionalists, or others to stop individuals making strong links across cultural boundaries. In other words, it promotes a more equal distribution of resources, opportunities and attention among individuals and families irrespective of their linguistic affiliation. The eventual outcome of a democratic culture might be the dissolution of strong cultural boundaries between groups within the society. By contrast, a democracy of cultures would tend to strengthen those boundaries. It may be argued that in an unequal multicultural society a democracy of cultures is, in practice, a necessary condition for the eventual emergence of a democratic culture. For example, it would tend to undermine formal or informal barriers to opportunity which derive from the systematic denigration of certain cultures and languages. However, a democracy of cultures may give undue influence to leaders within language communities whose particular interests may set them against any weakening of boundaries among cultures. Such opposition to cultural interpenetration can be a barrier to individual opportunity within an open capitalist democracy. In other words, even if a democracy of cultures is a necessary condition for the strengthening of a democratic culture, it may not be a sufficient condition and could even become an effective obstacle to achieving that goal.[5]

The third set of issues raised by Clyne's paper follows from his observations on the resistance of high-status groups to the advantage conferred in school examinations in languages to second-generation bilingual young Australians. More specifically, there is some pressure to adjust downwards the marks of candidates who speak the language being examined at home (e.g. Vietnamese) and who, therefore, have an advantage denied others. This is a fascinating variation on Pierre Bourdieu's more general argument about cultural capital within education systems.[6] As Clyne points out, and Bourdieu would presumably agree, students with family backgrounds giving them easy access to and familiarity with music, theatre or other aspects of 'high culture' have an advantage in those aspects of the curriculum. This advantage produces additional marks in certain examinations, a fact that is taken for granted rather than being penalised. Some interesting questions are raised by a comparison between the treatment of the cultural capital of, on the one hand, say, a Parisian surgeon's daughter in the French education system and a Vietnamese shop-keeper's daughter in the Australian education system. Why is the advantage enjoyed by the former generally accepted while the advantage enjoyed by the latter becomes the object of dispute?

One important variable may be the relative degree of unity, strength and hegemonic capacity[7] of the cultural establishment in each society. If Australian society has a weaker, less unified and less hegemonic cultural establishment than France, different cultural interests, for example, different language communities, would have a greater chance of altering the perceived value of their cultural capital by positive action of some kind. Resistance to such strategies by groups who would suffer a worsening of their position would be equally overt and direct. The dispute over marking languages examinations in the Australian case may illustrate conflicting pressures of this kind. More generally, the rank order of different cultural capitals seems more fluid and changeable in Australia than France. One relevant factor may be that upward valuation of cultural capital is easier to achieve when that capital is explicitly tied to ethnicity (Chinese, Japanese, Greek, etc.) rather than social class. A language community whose leaders have property, education and some standing in business or the professions has more chance of being influential at the points where resource decisions are made than a working class interest which has little organisational capacity within the relevant institutional spheres.

Finally, Clyne's reference to the political scientist Donald Horne on the final page of his paper reminds me of Horne's book *The Public Culture* (Horne, 1986). By this term Horne means a shared, visible culture, expressed in the symbols transmitted overtly or covertly, intentionally or not, in a society's mass media, architecture, leisure activities including shopping and other 'collective habits' (p. 56). The formal educational curriculum is, in that sense, also part of the 'public culture', an important symbol of what knowledge the society values and how it ranks this knowledge. Two warnings given by Horne are relevant. One is that symbolic victories at the level of the public culture, for example, getting specific languages onto the formal curriculum, do not in themselves undermine racial or ethnic discrimination in day-to-day interaction on the streets and in the work place. The other warning is that within a modern society a balance has to be struck between, on the one hand, the rights and functions of minorities and, on the other, the symbolic power and integrating capacity of the public culture. Horne writes that 'A true multi-ethnicity would mean the end of a public culture' (p. 207). That point can be strengthened by emphasising the particular dilemma raised by any language policy which encourages the creation and maintenance of a strong democracy of cultures, one in which each language community occupies its own room within an Australian Tower of Babel. This situation may produce advantages for Australian businesses trading within the Pacific region but will the cost be a reduction in the capacity of Australians from different linguistic backgrounds to speak to each other, to negotiate with each other within a shared national culture? Can we adapt Horne's phrase and say that 'A truly multilingual Australia would mean the end of an integrated Australian public culture'?

Acknowledgement

I am grateful for the comments of Sue Wright on earlier drafts of this paper.

Notes

1. In the United States, the transition of 'foreign' immigrants (European, Latin American, Asian and so on) from inner-city ethnic enclaves to the American way of life in the suburbs over two or three generations has become highly institutionalised. This transition is experienced as an 'upward' movement, initially by the ethnic communities as a whole, later by individual families who leave their ethnic preoccupations behind, except on special days of celebration (e.g. St Patrick's Day) as they 'become American'. Is there any equivalent institutionalised process of transition whereby families whose roots are within ethnic enclaves 'become Australian' over a number of generations? Is it possible to retain cultural diversity and multiple identity without institutionalising them as aspects of a process which is continually preparing individuals and groups for full participation in a shared Australian identity?

2. See issue of *Current Issues in Language and Society* (1994) 1 (2), on 'Experiences in the Netherlands and Belgium'.

3. While the United States may eventually move in a 'Belgian' direction, the advantages currently enjoyed by English speakers in the United States (as elsewhere) are not lost on French-speaking elements in Belgium. They therefore support efforts to build up the position of French as a language with equivalent European and global influence. The stronger the position of French within Europe and beyond, the stronger the position of the Walloon interest within Belgium.

4. During the 1930s and 1940s Elias did not share Arendt's enthusiasm for Zionism. The comparison between Elias and Arendt is developed in Smith (1997).

5. Some interesting choices confront Australian society in this context. Australians are competing within a region in which forces sustaining the solidarity of language communities, such as strong family ties, are mobilised as a positive asset, as the basis of a flexible and innovative 'Confucian capitalism' which places the interests of the extended kinship group above those of the individual. Should the communal

solidarities of 'new' Australians from the Pacific region be treated as an asset rather than a threat? See, for example, Dore (1987).
6. For example, in Bourdieu and Passeron (1977: 73–83; Bourdieu (1988), especially Chapter 3; Bourdieu (1996): 88–9.
7. By 'hegemonic capacity' is meant the capacity of a cultural establishment to ensure that its values pervade the key institutional sectors and social groups within the polity, both centrally and locally.

References

Bourdieu, P. (1988) *Homo Academicus*. Cambridge: Polity.
Bourdieu, P. (1996) *The State Nobility*. Cambridge: Polity.
Bourdieu, P. and Passeron, J-C. (1977) *Reproduction in Education, Society and Culture*. London: Sage.
Dore, R.P. (1987) *Taking Japan Seriously. A Confucian Perspective on Leading Economic Issues*. London: The Athlone Press.
Holli, M. (1981) The Great War sinks Chicago's German kultur. In M. Holli and P. d'A. Jones (eds) *Ethnic Chicago*. Grand Rapids, Michigan: Wm B. Eerdmans.
Horne, D. (1986) *The Public Culture*. London: Pluto Press.
Lo Bianco, J. (1987) Making language policy: Australia's experience. In R.B. Baldauf and A. Luke (eds) (1987) *Language Planning and Education in Australasia and the South Pacific* (pp. 47–79). Clevedon: Multilingual Matters.
Smith, D. (1997) Civilization and totalitarianism. A comparison of Norbert Elias and Hannah Arendt. Paper presented to the Annual Conference of the American Sociological Association, Toronto, August 1997.
Smolicz, J.J. *et al.*, (1984) *Education for a Cultural Democracy*. Adelaide: Task Force to investigate Multiculturalism and Education.

Just How Safe is Australia's Multilingual Language Policy? A Response to Michael Clyne

Stephen May

Sociology Department, University of Bristol, 12 Woodland Road, Bristol BS8 1UQ

The multilingual language and education policies adopted in Australia over the last two decades are viewed with considerable envy by those of us who are concerned with promoting more pluralistic policies in our own nation-states. Much of the credit for the progress made in Australia must go to Michael Clyne, and other prominent advocates like Smolicz and Lo Bianco, who have been so influential in promoting and subsequently shaping these policies. The advances achieved here are all the more remarkable, given the prior long-held intransigence in Australia to *any* formal recognition of cultural and linguistic diversity; an antagonism to minority cultures and languages most prominently exemplified in the racist White Australia Policy.

But as the rapid transformation of Australia's language policies has been spectacular, so too might be their demise. Indeed, signs of the latter are already ominously present. And it is this concern that I want to address in my response to Michael Clyne's stimulating and informed account on the current state of play there. Clyne avers that multilingualism/multiculturalism are now quite secure in Australia. I am not so sure, and there are a number of tensions that run through Clyne's account which would seem to reinforce a greater degree of scepticism than he admits.

For a start, there is a tension at the heart of Clyne's analysis between the development of a multilingual language policy as part of an emergent, more pluralistic Australian identity, and one that is dictated by the tenets of economic rationalism. The National Policy on Languages (NPL: Lo Bianco, 1987) represents the former while the Australian Language and Literacy Policy (ALLP: Dawkins, 1991) reflects the latter. What is clear from both Clyne's account and elsewhere (see Ozolins, 1993; Herriman, 1996), is that the NPL's broad concern with ethnic identity, language rights, and language diversity as a social, cultural and economic resource has been *eclipsed* by the far narrower economic-rationalist tenets reflected in the ALLP document. One might even go so far as to say that the latter document formed the vanguard of Keating's 'Productive Diversity' policy. There are strengths to this, as Clyne points out — notably, the argument concerning the economic collateral attached to promoting Asian languages within Australia as a contact point for trade, diplomacy and tourism. However, the economic argument is always a two-edged sword. After all, what may be today's feted market destination may be tomorrow's political nemesis. More significantly, economic arguments do little, if anything, to secure the notion of multilingualism as a *right*, a feature that was central to the NPL. The exigencies of trade and politics (both internal and external) — the influence of the 'market', in effect — provide no ongoing guarantees or even continuity in this regard (see below). Moreover, the criterion of placing economic value on languages works far more to the *dis*advantage of minority languages than to their advantage. One only needs to look at the current hegemony of English, and the 'linguistic genocide' (Day, 1985) that it has wreaked on minority languages, to see this.

This brings me to a second tension in Clyne's analysis. The economic argument may serve to promote minority languages which have some 'instrumental' value elsewhere but it does nothing to support the value of national and indigenous minority languages which are spoken nowhere else. Indeed, an economic-rationalist argument directly militates against the ongoing survival of such languages. When this is allied with the cultural and social stigma often attached to national minority languages, the situation is even bleaker. The fate of Aboriginal languages provides us with a salutary example here. When Australia was annexed to Britain in 1770 more than 250 languages were used by different Aboriginal communities in Australia. Some 200 years on only 90 of these languages remain in use, with 70 of these threatened with extinction in the near future. Only about 10% of Aboriginal peoples still speak indigenous languages, that is, 30,000 out of 300,000 (Brenzinger, 1997). Suffice it to say, that economic arguments do nothing to ameliorate this situation; in fact, they tend only to entrench it further. As Crawford (1994) notes, language death seldom occurs in communities of wealth and privilege, but rather to the dispossessed and disempowered.

A third tension is that which exists between the use of minority languages in the public and private domains. It is true that the multilingual language policies adopted in Australia have fostered the use of minority languages in the private domain and this, in itself, is a significant achievement. However, there is little to suggest beyond this. In this regard, Australia continues to reflect the widely held nationalist principle of a common (public) language as a central pillar of the nation-state (Gellner, 1983; Anderson, 1991). The result is that all significant activities conducted in the public domain remain resolutely monolingual. Concomitantly, linguistic shift, as Clyne points out, proceeds largely unabated while minority language use remains limited to a few restricted (low status) domains. This situation does little to foster the status and use of minority languages. Indeed, it may lead to the reverse. The limitation of a language to particular domains can mean the social and political impoverishment and marginalisation of the language concerned. Given the spread of standardised education, the associated literacy demands of the labour force, and the inevitable and widespread interaction required in dealing with state agencies, any language which is not widely used in the public realm becomes so marginalised as to be inconsequential (Kymlicka, 1995). It is only when minority languages are *legitimated* by the state and *institutionalised* in the public realm (Nelde *et al.*, 1996; May, in preparation) that this state of affairs begins to change. Australia — like most nation-states — is still a long way from achieving this.

Which brings me to my final caution in response to Clyne's paper. Debates on minority language policy are always embedded within wider social, economic and political contexts, along with the hegemonic power relations that underlie these. And it is this issue of power relations which seems to me to have been insufficiently addressed here. The recent development of multilingual language and education policies in Australia has been hard fought and hard won to be sure and, again, their merits are to be acclaimed. But their ongoing fragility is also clearly apparent. This is evidenced by the recent shift to a more economic-rationalist account of language policy formulation, already discussed. However, even more serious are the recent political changes in Australia which have seen: (1) a return, post-Keating, to a more overtly assimilationist stance at the level of government; and (2) the concomitant rise and popularisation of racist rhetoric against Aboriginal peoples and Asian migrants, most notably represented by Pauline Hanson's 'One Nation' Party. The latter is not to my mind just a passing fad, as Clyne suggests, but reflects the underlying structural racism which is a legacy of Australia's heritage as a white settler colony. In this light, these events point to the *contest* and *conflict* that any recognition of minority languages (and the ethnicities to which they attach) precipitates. Multilingual language and education policies are, and will remain contentious, simply because they may necessitate changes, within a given nation-state, to the balance of wider power relations between ethnic groups and the languages they speak. Australia is certainly now a multi-ethnic nation-state, of that there is no doubt. But given the ongoing ascendancy of the white 'Anglo-Celtic' majority in Australia, and the current political climate, the degree to which this ethnic and linguistic diversity continues to be reflected in a multicultural/multilingual public policy is far less assured.

References

Anderson, B. (1991) *Imagined Communities: Reflections on the Origin and Spread of Nationalism* (revised edn). London: Verso.

Brenzinger, M. (1997) Language contact and language displacement. In F. Coulmas (ed.) *The Handbook of Sociolinguistics* (pp. 273–84). Oxford: Blackwell.

Crawford, J. (1994) Endangered Native American languages: What is to be done and why? *Journal of Navajo Education* 11 (3), 3–11.

Dawkins, J. (1991) *Australia's Language: The Australian Language and Literacy Policy.* Canberra: Australian Government Publishing Service.

Day, R. (1985) The ultimate inequality: Linguistic genocide. In N. Wolfson and J. Manes (eds) *Language of Inequality* (pp. 163–81). Berlin: Mouton de Gruyter.

Gellner, E. (1983) *Nations and Nationalism: New Perspectives on the Past.* Oxford: Basil Blackwell.

Herriman, M. (1996) Language policy in Australia. In M. Herriman and B. Burnaby (eds) *Language Policies in English-Dominant Countries* (pp. 35–61). Clevedon: Multilingual Matters.

Kymlicka, W. (1995) *Multicultural Citizenship: A Liberal Theory of Minority Rights.* Oxford: Clarendon Press.

Lo Bianco, J. (1987) *National Policy on Languages.* Commonwealth Department of Education, Canberra: AGPS.

May, S. (In preparation) Re-imagining the Nation-state: Language, education and minority rights.

Nelde, P., Strubell, M. and Williams, G. (1996) *Euromosaic: The Production and Reproduction of the Minority Language Groups in the European Union.* Luxembourg. Office for Official Publications of the European Communities.

Ozolins, U. (1993) *The Politics of Language in Australia.* Cambridge: Cambridge University Press.

Michael Clyne comments:

I agree about the social rationale for language diversity being eclipsed by the economic rationale, but this is what is dominating all government policy, most notably in education and public health, not just in language. So, right-wing leaders like Kennett, the Victorian Premier, are condemning Hanson not only for trying to disrupt the harmony but particularly for damaging trade with Asia.

There is a danger that we have now lost the plot in relation to language policy. The universal public condemnation of the Green Paper preceding the Australian Language and Literacy Policy meant that the latter had to contain an endorsement of the principles of the National Policy on Languages. No-one consults the public about policy changes these days. One of the most unfortunate aspects of ALLP was the introduction of a false dichotomy of language and literacy which ignores the fact that literacy relates to language (not to a particular language). Some 'educational experts' (management and not literacy experts) have argued recently that our 'deplorable' literacy standards cannot be improved because the primary school curriculum is now crowded with new areas such as languages other than English!

On domains of community language use not being 'high status', does that not depend on the interpretation by the group? Religion and education are regarded as very high status BY?? some communities.

Probably the achievement of the Australian developments has been the opportunity to express multiple identity culturally and linguistically without being excluded from belonging to the nation.

Who Maintains/Relinquishes Which Language How and Why? A Response to Michael Clyne

Li Wei
Department of Speech, King George VI Building, University of Newcastle upon Tyne NE1 7RU, UK

In reviewing over 30 years of research on societal multilingualism, Fishman (1991) suggests that there are three key aspects which an 'informed evaluation' of language maintenance and language shift (LMLS) should consider: habitual language use, behaviour towards language, and socio-cultural change processes. He argues that most progress has been made in conjunction with the measurement of habitual language use, or in his famous question 'Who Speaks What Language to Whom and When', and least in conjunction with socio-cultural change processes. This, in Fishman's opinion, 'reflects the greater precision of scholarly work with language as a result of the more highly systematic nature of language and language behaviour', while the 'social sciences in general and sociology in particular simply have not reached the same level of precise and systematic analysis' (1989: 253). Whether or not one accepts Fishman's assertion, the only coherent analytic model which has been widely used in the study of LMLS has been Fishman's *domain analysis* which focuses on the habitual language use of individual speakers. In contrast, no similar model is available for analysing the socio-cultural processes associated with LMLS. Research to date has been concerned primarily with isolating those factors which accelerate language shift from those which inhibit it and favour maintenance. While such lists of factors may help clarify what contributes to LMLS, they have little to say about the relative importance of the various factors, or about how individual speakers and their communities respond to macro-level societal pressures. What seems to be needed is an integrated approach which addresses the social, political and economic change processes at large as well as the ways in which individual speakers deal with the changes in everyday interaction.

An integrated model of LMLS requires comparative analyses of the sociolinguistic practices of different communities. There are two broad types of comparative studies in the existing literature — large scale, multi-national comparisons, and comparisons in one country or region across a number of communities or even within one community across different generations and groups of speakers. It can be argued that the latter type of small-scale comparisons may be more useful than the large-scale cross-nation ones, as they can offer us more information on how and why the same conditions have affected different groups in different ways. Michael Clyne's work on language maintenance of the various communities in Australia, as reported in the focus paper in this volume, is an excellent example of comparative analysis. It is not merely a descriptive account of who speaks what language to whom and when, but a more critical evaluation of 'who maintains/relinquishes which language how and why'. I shall now comment on some of the key issues emerging from Clyne's paper and add further examples from other communities.

Who?

The most obvious question in LMLS research is who has maintained the traditional community language and who has given it up in favour of some other language(s). Research to date has repeatedly found that there are age-related patterns of LMLS; in other words, older speakers tend to maintain the traditional language better than do younger speakers. While correlations between age and patterns of language use provide some of the clearest evidence of LMLS in specific communities, they are the least interesting findings of all, because all they can tell us is that the community in question has changed its patterns of language use. They have almost nothing to say about the social, political, economic and linguistic reasons for the change to take place. Moreover, many more detailed studies have revealed that speakers of the same age groups do not always behave linguistically in the same manner at all times. 'Atypical' speakers and 'atypical' patterns can easily be found in all domains. Our studies of the Cantonese-English bilingual community in Tyneside in the north-east of England, for example, discovered a number of 'anomalous' speakers whose language choice patterns are very different from those of similar age in their generation (e.g. Li Wei *et al.*, 1992; Li Wei, 1994; Milroy & Li Wei, 1995). We have tried to explain the apparent anomaly in terms of the social network patterns of individual speakers. Similarly, Clyne and his associates, most notably Pauwels (1995; 1997), have shown that women and men of the same age group often display different language choice patterns.

This last issue — gender differentiations in LMLS — brings me to my second question about which language speakers maintain or relinquish.

Which Language?

This is in fact a highly complex issue, but somehow it has not received much attention in the existing literature on LMLS. In relation to gender, there have been contradictory findings. Some suggests that women in bilingual communities lead the shift, usually from the minority language to the majority language when there is clear social differentiation between the languages co-available in the community; others seem to suggest that women in ethnic minority communities tend to maintain their 'ethnic' language more than men. Some of the contradiction and confusion can be explained reasonably easily, if the researchers provide sufficient information about the overall sociolinguistic structure of the communities in question. For instance, in some communities women's higher level of language maintenance is a matter of monolingualism, i.e. they have not acquired the 'majority' language for a variety of reasons. Such a situation would be very different from one in which the women are bilinguals and continue to use the ethnic language more than their male counterparts. In other communities, however, the question is not simply whether women maintain the traditional community language or replace it with a different language, but which language they actually maintain or relinquish.

We have recently carried out a small survey, as part of a larger, on-going research project, on the Hakka-speaking families in Newcastle upon Tyne and have found that all of the 14 Hakka-first-language-speaking women we have studied have acquired Cantonese, the lingua franca of the Chinese community in Britain, and use it regularly in social interaction, but only three of them claimed to be able to speak English. However, only three out of the nine Hakka-first-language-speaking men whom we studied have acquired Cantonese, yet all of them can speak English. Furthermore, all the children of the Hakka-speaking families that we have studied have acquired Cantonese and English, although only six out of a total of 22 claimed to be able to speak Hakka.

Findings of the kind presented here would naturally raise the question 'why?', but there is one further question which is often missed out in LMLS research and which needs to be addressed before we can adequately address the why question: how one language replaces another as the dominant language in a community and how one language manages to maintain its dominant role despite all the socio-linguistic pressures?

How?

The how question can be dealt with at different levels. At the societal level, we can examine how multilingualism is managed through legislation and/or educational provisions. What may be particularly interesting here is to see how different languages are treated differently. In Britain, for example, not all the Asian languages and varieties of Chinese which are routinely used in the community receive institutional support. GCSE and A-Level examinations are available for Urdu, Hindi, Punjabi, Cantonese and Mandarin, but not others, despite the fact that some of these, for instance, Mandarin, have only a very small number of native speakers in the country. At the community level, the transmission of particular languages has long been an issue of concern, and sometimes conflict. As far as the Chinese community is concerned, Hakka, which has the second largest native-speaker population in the UK, is never formally taught in the community schools, whereas Mandarin, a language variety which is officially recognised by all the Chinese-speaking countries (e.g. China, Taiwan and Singapore) is being promoted alongside Cantonese. Furthermore, the how question can be dealt with at an individual level — how does the socio-cultural change that is taking place in the community come to be interpreted by the speakers themselves in a way that affects their everyday language use? Research evidence shows that the ways in which different speakers and speaker groups deal with LMLS lead to linguistic innovations, structural changes, and new varieties of language.

Why?

No research on LMLS is complete without addressing the why question, of course. For a long time, investigators have focused their efforts on finding (ultimately universal) patterns of causality. Social changes such as industrialisation, urbanisation, and government policies have been suggested as responsible for a group giving up its traditional language use pattern. However, as Kulick (1992: 9) points out, to evoke macro-sociological change as a *cause* of language shift is 'to leave out the crucial step of understanding how that change has come to be interpreted by the people it is supposed to be influencing'. Kulick argues that shift in language use is caused by shifts in personal and group values and goals. What urbanisation or industrialisation may do to people is to lead them to revise their perceptions of themselves and their world, or, in more familiar terminology, their attitudes, and these revisions may eventually lead to their change of language use. Far too often, work on language shift has concentrated on examining the end result of change. The process of the change, i.e. 'why and how do people come to interpret their own identity in such a way that they abandon their language in favour of another language?' has not received enough of the attention it clearly deserves.

Since Fishman's seminal paper in 1964, LMLS has become a pivotal topic in sociolinguistic research. There now exists a large body of literature documenting the linguistic fortunes of a range of communities in different parts of the world. Nevertheless, the analytic approach to the topic has remained predominantly the one originally proposed by Fishman, which takes LMLS as a by-product of higher-level, power-related social processes. The capacity of individual speakers to make use of the linguistic and social resources available to them in producing and reproducing social structures and social order is often underestimated. LMLS is a complex and dynamic process. It involves people rethinking their identities, goals and values. LMLS research should therefore be a 'study of a people's conceptions of themselves in relation to one another and to their changing social world, and of how those conceptions are encoded by and mediated through language' (Kulick, 1992: 9). Viewed in this way, LMLS research should not be a merely descriptive discipline but a more evaluative, even critical, area of social science.

Acknowledgements

My thanks go to Vanitha Saravanan, Xu Daming, Dom Watt and Zhu Hua for discussing some of the ideas in this paper and for commenting on an earlier draft. The study of Hakka-speaking families mentioned in the paper is part of an ESRC funded research project (R000 23 5869).

Notes

1. Regional language varieties.

References

Fishman, J. (1989) *Language and Ethnicity in Minority Sociolinguistic Perspective*. Clevedon: Multilingual Matters.
Fishman, J. (1991) *Reversing Language Shift*. Clevedon: Multilingual Matters.
Kulick, D. (1992) *Language Shift and Cultural Reproduction*. Cambridge: Cambridge University Press.
Li Wei, Milroy, L. and Pong, S.C. (1992) A two-step sociolinguistic analysis of code-switching and language choice. *International Journal of Applied Linguistics* 2, 63–85.
Li Wei (1994) *Three Generations Two Languages One Family*. Clevedon: Multilingual Matters.
Milroy, L. and Li Wei (1995) A social network approach to code-switching. In L. Milroy, and P. Muysken (eds) *One Speaker Two Languages* (pp. 136–57). Cambridge: Cambridge University Press.
Pauwels, A. (1995) Linguistic practices and language maintenance among bilingual women and men in Australia. *Nordlyd* 23, 21–50.
Pauwels, A. (1997) The role of gender in immigrant language maintenance in Australia. In W. Wolck and A. De Houwer (eds) *Recent Studies in Contact Linguistics*, 276–85.

Michael Clyne comments:

We have also found that Chinese groups are quite instrumental in their motivation to replace languages, so that, while some Hakka and other *fangyan*[1] speakers adopt both Cantonese and English as their lingua francas, others shift from Cantonese to English and Mandarin.

I find Li Wei's schema very useful and also agree that too often the process of language shift is not followed but is simply deduced from the product.

The Case for Economic Considerations in Language Policy Making: A Response to Michael Clyne

Vanithamani Saravanan
Nanyang Technological University, National Institute of Education, School of Arts, English Language and Applied Linguistics, 469, Bukit Timah Road, Singapore 25975

One of the main themes in Clyne's paper on multilingualism and multiculturalism in Australia is the value of language resources to the nation as a whole. He states that language resources enrich the nation as well as the individual because they relate to issues of social justice, as well as to long term economic strategies and cultural enrichment for all Australians. Clyne notes that the broader links that education used to have in Australia with media and public services have given way to an emphasis on labour market needs.

Other researchers too have observed the place of economic considerations in language planning. Edwards (1994) observes that pragmatic and economic considerations are of central importance. He refers to Dorian's work where Dorian observes the declining fortunes of Scottish Gaelic and states that language loyalty persists as long as economic and social circumstances are conducive to it, but if some other language proves to have greater value, a shift to that other language begins. Edwards further states that formal language planning itself can do little to counter the language shift caused by the (usually desirable) processes of urbanisation, modernisation and mobility.

Singapore provides an interesting case in terms of its educational and language planning policies and their direct links to manpower training. In Singapore, the politicians and administrators have always linked education with manpower training, since human resources training is seen as essential and crucial in a country with virtually no natural resources. In a paper on 'Globalisation, the state and education policy in Singapore' Gopinathan (1997: 71) states that Singapore's educational policy environment can best be understood within its larger social-political context. Singapore society in the 1950s was characterised by deep ethnic and linguistic segmentation. It was poor, had a rapidly rising birth rate, and few prospects for economic survival. A legacy of the British colonial period was a segmented educational school system that mirrored a segmented Singapore society.

Manpower training for a market economy has not been the only consideration in national educational policies in Singapore. Other national goals include ways of unifying about 20 disparate linguistic groups as well as diverse cultural and religious communities into a more cohesive nation. At the same time the recognition of diversity has led to support for the maintenance of the heritage of the different linguistic and cultural communities. But instead of providing resources for all linguistic communities, policy making was governed by what has been described as 'effective management of language resources' (Gopi-nathan, 1994).

The Singapore government decided that there was a need to select and develop particular languages. Thus language planning decisions led to the deployment of resources to spread and strengthen English language education as English hastened the processes of urbanisation, modernisation and mobility. Three other languages, namely Mandarin, Tamil and Malay, were selected as mother tongue languages. Although there are no specific language planning agencies in Singapore, policy decisions are institutionalised through the Ministry of Educa-tion and implemented through educational administrators and teachers in schools and in all educational institutions. Thus, in comparison with Australia, Singapore displays a setting where bilingualism and multiligualism are institu-tionalised as the domains of the various language users and uses have been determined by these policy decisions taken over a period of 30 years.

Clyne argues that mainstreaming bilingualism in Australia has not produced the diversity and variety expected from multiculturalism. In Singapore main-streaming bilingualism has similarly meant decisions were taken to select some languages for state support as well as well as community support. It meant the selection of, for example, English and its inevitable strengthening in particular domains, such as government, education, business, work, etc. Mandarin was preferred over other Chinese languages, Hokkien, Teochew, Cantonese, the mother tongues of many Singaporean Chinese, termed 'dialects' by the govern-ment. The rationale was to use Mandarin, a high status standard variety taught in schools from the early 1950s, to unify the various Chinese communities — a role seen as legitimate. There was concern that if the Chinese 'dialects' persisted, the Chinese-speaking communities would remain fragmented and that English would become a lingua franca within the Chinese community (Gopinathan, 1994: 71). It is these decisions taken in the economic and social management of human resources, the government argues, which give Singapore its political and social stability, and at the same time ensure ethnic and cultural diversity and social harmony.

Institutionalising the four official languages meant the provision of funding for educational needs — teacher training, preparation of curriculum materials and the maintenance of school based literacy programmes. Apart from meeting these mainstream educational needs, there was also a need for the allocation of resources for media, radio, television, newspapers, as well as arts, cultural and heritage programmes, for example, funding and supporting Chinese music, dance, drama, folklore and folk culture activities such as martial arts, lion and folk dance troupes, folk opera, Chinese Symphony Orchestras, Chinese calligra-phy and brush painting. Similarly there is support for Indian and Malay classical and folk cultural programmes. In all, this meant sustaining and maintaining linguistic and cultural programmes in all four languages, for all age groups, both school age and adult, so that both community heritage and nation-building went hand in hand. The government saw the potential of English language education in the service of rapid industrialisation and modernisation, in the development of a market economy, as a contribution to Singapore's growth as the service centre of the region, and in transforming the country into a city state. It did not take long to persuade Singapore parents that an investment in their children's education, an education in the medium of English with an education in mother tongue language and values would give their children the necessary qualifications and skills as a means towards better career opportunities in competitive jobs and that this in turn would lead to better lives when compared to their forefathers who had suffered years of hardship and penury. It was argued that when people are educated and skilled they become the national assets of their country and that the national wealth accrued will in turn be translated to economic assets for the people.

Clyne observes that the stress in Australia on economic rationalism in selecting language policies has created a case of cultural democracy versus economic rationalism. Singapore again provides an interesting case for comparison. The place of mother tongue education was to give each ethnic community in Singapore access to their distinctive cultural roots and heritage and the great classical literatures of the various cultures and civilizations. During the 1980s, however, the opening of markets in China and burgeoning contacts with that country quickly led Singapore to recognise the economic value of Mandarin. The government seized these opportunities for Singaporeans to become, in a sense, the bilingual brokers between the West and China. Over the years, links with China have been developed and Singapore has taken advantage of *'guanxi'* or networking — translated literally as the natural links that exist in terms of linguistic and cultural ties, including ways of doing business. Many Chinese Singaporeans have been motivated to take up training courses in business Chinese.

These contacts with China have led to numerous business ventures as well as the building of whole new towns and industrial parks by Singaporean business-men and workers. Thus the economic benefits of a language policy that was motivated by economic rationalism came about 20–30 years later. While Singaporean Chinese attend courses in business Mandarin, their Chinese counterparts come to Singapore to attend management courses taught in Mandarin. What this has done is to create an expansion of functions for the use of both oral and written Mandarin, from the drawing up of legal documents and business contracts, through the use of Mandarin as a medium for training professional staff and workers, to day-to-day interaction in the language.

Similarly, attempts have been made to provide an economic rationale behind the provision of Tamil and Malay. Recently there has been a move to link the Tamil language with doing business in Tamil Nadu.

Singapore is in the process of setting up joint projects with Indians in Bangalore, the silicon valley of India. There is therefore the potential of using English and other regional languages such as Tamil and Telugu for joint business initiatives. Note that a recent decision has been to allow and support and recognise community based language classes in Hindi, Punjabi, Bengali, Gujerati and Urdu. These languages may be offered for all levels of the national examinations. Malay as the regional language of Malaysia, Sarawak, Sabah, Brunei and Indonesia has received further impetus and gained economic currency with the expansion of joint ventures with all these countries, Malay has gained greater prestige among Singaporean Malays and non-Malays who speak Malay.

Finally, we should recognise that various linguistic communities in Singapore have experienced language shift as a result of policy makers selecting only particular languages for official support. However, even those communities given official support have experienced some shift, with some being more affected than others (Saravanan, 1996). The Chinese community, the Tamil community and to a smaller extent the Malay communities have each experienced shift. One explanation that can be offered for this is the fact that English has become associated with economic and social mobility. The other explanation relates to the policy of 'cost effectiveness' which the government has used to justify numerous policies affecting education, housing, health etc. But whether in doing so there has been adequate consideration of social management of human resources that will ensure diversity and social harmony is something that the government will have to review periodically. Accommodation to the various community demands and the needs of non-English speaking groups is one of the ways in which the government has sought to avoid serious conflict.

Clyne makes reference to the Australian context where the expression and sharing of individual language, religion and cultural heritage is seen as a right. Singapore has maintained pluralism through support for the various languages, cultures and religions of the various communities. It has also used its educational institutions to develop the nation as a civic community rooted in a common core of shared values. But, at the same time there is no institutional support for all the home languages spoken by Singaporeans. Various communities, like the Malayali Indian community have had to seek their own resources and apply their own energies to develop small-scale mother-tongue language and culture programmes. The selection of languages, the development and spread of English has contributed to the cultural hegemony of English in both public and private domains.

What of the mother tongues of the various Chinese communities in the 1990s? A recent study (Li Wei *et al.*, 1997) of the Teochew Chinese speaking community (22.1% of the Chinese-speaking population) concluded that many young Teochew speakers no longer identify themselves as Teochews but as Singaporean Chinese or simply as Singaporeans. Parents who could speak Teochew used it with older members of the family, but otherwise regarded Mandarin and English as the normal languages for wider communication. For example, the main language of communication that parents chose to use with their children, and with members of their own generation was Mandarin. Commenting on their Teochew identity, speakers said that there were more important indicators of identity such as family, descent, food, festivals. They had, therefore, put the instrumental value of Mandarin and English before the symbolic value of Teochew.

It has been observed that in time the spread of Mandarin amongst a majority Chinese speaking population of 77% will contribute to the cultural hegemony of Mandarin in certain public and private domains. This year's 'Speak Mandarin' campaign 'Speak Mandarin, explore new horizons' is targeted at English-educated Singaporeans. Activities include the use of Chinese web sites, multimedia tools such as CD-ROMs of games and stories from Chinese classics, the promotion of Chinese resources on the Internet as part of the Chinese language curriculum in schools, as well as introducing English-educated Chinese Singaporeans to Chinese language Internet websites.

At this year's national day rally the prime minister spoke of developing a core group of Chinese Singaporeans steeped in Chinese culture, history, literature and the arts. Current discussion refers to further accommodation to Chinese organisations wanting to strengthen the political and social contributions of the Chinese-educated. The Chinese Teachers' Union has asked for a Higher Chinese syllabus and textbooks which will convey Chinese cultural values and heritage. The government has supported these suggestions by announcing further educational measures to help in the development of a Chinese elite from the Chinese educated, as well as supporting the development of a Tamil-educated and a Malay-educated elite. The deputy prime minister, Lee Hsien Loong, was reported in the *Straits Times* (4 September 1997) as saying that the future Chinese elite will come from a core of students who not only have mastery of Chinese for utilitarian purposes but who will also have internalised Chinese cultural values and heritage.

A review of educational policies from primary through secondary to tertiary levels is currently being carried out with international consultants. The purpose is to make changes to the educational system and to review manpower training, to make these areas relevant to an international market economy brought about by the globalisation of markets and financial institutions and the impetus from information technology. Of course, Singapore is not the only country that has been forced to review its educational policies and manpower training policies and respond to the globalisation of economic and financial institutions. Similar concerns are echoed in ministerial statements and newspaper reports from other parts of the region. For example, the *Straits Times* (19 September 1997) reports a leading Malay daily, *Utusan Malaysia*, as saying that English is vital for the progress of Malaysia as it is a language of knowledge — a point emphasised by the prime minister of Malaysia, Mahatir Mohammed. And besides English, Malay students should gradually be taught Mandarin as China is poised to dominate the global arena.

Economic considerations in language policy making will continue to remain one of the main concerns in small, developed nation states such as Singapore, if it is to continue with the establishment of stable policies which will ensure its stability and growth over the millennium.

References

Edwards, J. (1994) *Multilingualism*. London: Routledge.

Gopinathan, S. (1994) Language policy changes 1979–1992: Politics and pedagogy. In S. Gopinathan, A. Pakir., W.K. Ho and V. Saravanan (eds) *Language, Society and Education in Singapore: Issues and Trends*. Singapore: Times Academic Press.

Gopinathan, S. (1997) Globalisation, the state and education policy in Singapore. In W.O. Lee and Mark Bray (eds) *Education and Political Transition: Perspectives and Dimensions in East Asia (Comparative Educational Research Centre, Studies in Comparative Education)* (pp. 68–80). Hong Kong: University of Hong Kong.

Li Wei, Saravanan, V. and Ng Lee Hoon, J. (1997) Locating language shift in social space:

The case of the Teochew Community in Singapore. In W. Wölck and A. de Houwer (eds) *Plurilingua. Recent Studies in Contact Linguistics* (pp. 206–17). Bonn: Dummler.
Saravanan, V. (1996) Institutional attempts at language planning in Singapore: Sociolinguistic implications. In Jan Blommaert (ed.) *The Politics of Multilingualism and Language Planning. Antwerp Papers in Linguistics* no 87.

Michael Clyne comments:

The Singapore case is quite particular and a number of points need to be emphasised in relation to it. For example, the government has not only changed the 'mother tongues' of some families; through language usage, it has changed their perception of their 'language'. They have been led to believe that English is their first language, when really it is not, and that Hindi (the national language) is a dialect, while Tamil is the 'language' of the Indian Singaporeans. In fact, very few Singaporeans had Mandarin as a L1, and those Chinese with Hokkien or Hakka as their L1 had to believe that they did not speak such a language at home.

Uncertainty in the Community Language Classroom: A Response to Michael Clyne

Jane Stuart-Smith
Department of English Language, 12 University Gardens, University of Glasgow, Glasgow G12 8QQ, UK

One of the points that Clyne raises and rejects in his paper is the notion that learners of an 'ethnic background' have a particular advantage over learners with 'non-ethnic background', when learning a community language. His discussion refers particularly to the situation in Australia when children from an ethnic background, learning a community language in school alongside non-ethnic background learners, can be effectively penalised for their potential exposure to the language outside school. Here I would like to endorse Clyne's rejection of the supposed advantage held by ethnic background learners of a community language, by referring to evidence drawn from the learning and maintenance of Panjabi in the UK. I base my brief remarks both on my research and also on my own experience as a non-ethnic background learner of Panjabi.

Panjabi is a language subject which can be taken in school at GCSE Level (age 16 years) and at A Level (age 18 years). It is also maintained through more informal classes available for learners of all ages, but particularly children (aged from around six years), run either by the local authority, or from local Sikh temples. The form of Panjabi taught and examined (and referred to here) is the 'standard variety used for writing the language and by educated speakers' (Nagra, 1988: 4), written in the Gurmukhi script. It is associated with Sikhism; the Sikh holy book is largely written in an earlier form of the language.

The most striking area of disadvantage for the Panjabi learner of ethnic background in the UK context is the increasing distance between standard Panjabi and the language actually spoken by the community. By 'community' here, I am referring specifically to two very different communities of Panjabi speakers, mainly of Sikh religion, living in Oxford, and in West Birmingham; there is considerable diversity in both communities in terms of family migration history and linguistic background. Attempting a linguistic description of the 'community' language is difficult. It has its roots in a number of distinct geographical dialects of Panjabi spoken in the now Indian state of Panjab (including Majhi, Doabi, and Powadhi among others), with the addition of linguistic influences acquired from migration via East Africa. It has incorporated a large number of English words, and code-switching with English is also frequent (Romaine, 1985; 1995; Moffatt & Milroy, 1992; Stuart-Smith, 1997). We can say that many speakers regularly use a 'mixed' (or bilingual) Panjabi/English code (Romaine, 1995), which can vary in the degree of mixing (on attitudes to this, see Chana & Romaine, 1984; for the role of context, see Stuart-Smith, 1997).

The most obvious linguistic level where the standard and community varieties of Panjabi differ is lexical. This can be illustrated by comparing the vocabulary of basic introductory books on Panjabi for children (e.g. Nagra, 1984; Hemkunt, 1976), and the actual vocabulary of young second-generation children (Stuart-

Smith, 1997). As we might expect, the children frequently use English or mixed forms (e.g. dog for Pj. *kutta*, read *karna* for Pj. *parna*) for concepts expressed with Panjabi words in textbooks for beginners. The syntax of some children's speech is also starting to change with respect to the standard, for example, the more usual verb-final word order is giving way to subject-verb-object order. Phonological contrasts (of tone and retroflexion) are also changing in terms of their phonetic realisation, or being lost altogether (on tone, see Stuart-Smith and Cortina-Borja, forthcoming). Thus ethnic background learners of Panjabi, learning standard Panjabi taught in school or classes, cannot just reproduce their community language. Linguistic comparison suggests that they are tackling what is in many respects a different language.[1]

However it is not just the differences which could confuse learners with a background, the areas of similarity between the standard and community language might put these students at a disadvantage when compared with non-ethnic background learners. When studying for GCSE Panjabi, I (with no background) had few preconceptions about the language that I was learning. I would suggest that the situation is somewhat different for a speaker of community Panjabi, which is effectively a Panjabi/English bilingual code. In this case, the learner may be uncertain about those aspects of their language which overlap with the standard, and are thus useful for learning it, and those which will be deemed unacceptable, and so should be suppressed. This can introduce a high level of uncertainty into the language learning experience.

I witnessed such situations frequently whilst working at a Saturday morning Panjabi class for children and their parents (all of ethnic background). On one occasion I was helping to prepare a learner for the role plays required for the oral component of the GCSE exam, in which one side of the conversation is given. This fluent speaker of community Panjabi was thrown by the scripted responses, which she found unnatural, and the difficulty of replying in standard Panjabi. The gap between her own linguistic competence in the community language and that required for standard Panjabi left her less able to complete the task than I had been. A more serious problem for her, and other learners at the class, was understanding when the use of English words was acceptable in the standard language, since the taught standard does present a number of English loanwords (e.g. school, bus, bag). Our teacher herself was uncertain in many cases, which is not surprising, since the variety of Panjabi which she speaks most commonly herself is community Panjabi. Again, ethnic background learners found that accessing their linguistic experience was not always helpful for learning standard Panjabi. I, on the other hand, had simply learnt the vocabulary as it was presented to me, whether English or Panjabi, as 'Panjabi'.

I suggest then that learners of Panjabi in the UK with an ethnic background, like those learners of community languages in Australia, cannot be regarded as necessarily having an advantage over non-ethnic background learners.

Notes

1. The definition of language/dialect is of course a minefield of which I am only too
   aware.

References

Chana, U. and Romaine, S. (1984) Evaluative reactions to Panjabi/English code-switching. *Journal of Multilingual and Multicultural Development* 6, 447–73.

Hemkunt (1976) *Navin Panjabi Primer*. New Delhi: Hemkunt.

Moffatt, S. and L. Milroy (1992) Panjabi/English language alternation in the classroom in the early school years. *Multilingua* 11 (4), 355–84.

Nagra, J.S. (1984) *Panjabi Made Easy: Book 1*. Coventry: Nagra Publications.

Nagra, J.S. (1988) *GCSE Panjabi*. Coventry: Nagra Publications.

Romaine, S. (1985) *Language loss and maintenance in a multi-ethnic community*. Final report to ESRC on Grant HR8480.

Romaine, S. (1995) *Bilingualism* (2nd edn). Oxford: Blackwell.

Stuart-Smith, J. (1997) Code-switching and context: A school-based study of language alternation in 7 year old Panjabi/English bilingual children in Birmingham. Paper presented to the International Symposium of Bilingualism, Newcastle-upon-Tyne, UK, March 1997.

Stuart-Smith, J. and M. Cortina-Borja, (forthcoming) A preliminary investigation of tone in 'British' Panjabi. In *Proceedings of the XVIIIth South Asian Language Analysis Roundtable*. New Delhi: Motilal Banarsidass.

Michael Clyne comments:

Children with home backgrounds in the language they are studying do have some advantages, but these vary according to the background and they also have special needs that must be met for the advantages to be realised. Programmes have to address such matters.

Backlash: A Response to Michael Clyne

Dennis Ager
School of Languages and European Studies, Aston University, Aston Triangle, Birmingham B4 7ET

My aunt died recently in a hospital in England. Her daughter said: 'I suppose if she'd been black or Asian they might have done more'. A friend of mine, teaching in Victoria, Australia, said with some asperity that in order to implement the State's language policy the school was about to decide which of the ten other teachers in the school should be made redundant in order to recruit a German language teacher — German having been chosen because the only significant recent immigration to the (semi-rural) area had been of Germans in the 1930s, none of whom now spoke the language. Such 'backlash' anecdotes prove nothing, but they are live and personal examples of the phenomenon which Michael Clyne calls the 'negative association of the "advantaged" migrant': that is, a feeling by some in the host community that a migrant community is getting more than its fair share of resources. In the hands of politicians, such tales can be dynamite, even where they derive simply from a misunderstanding, and relating anecdotes is typical of the discourse of many extremists, not only in Australia but also in the rhetoric of such people as the French National Front leader Le Pen (Bréchon, 1994). Professor Clyne's search for an explanation of a possible 'end of the idyll' of accepted multiculturalism and multilingualism in the Australian National Policy on Languages suggests three political factors: the growth of economic rationalism, the educational explosion and changing definitions of (dis)advantage. The discussion of backlash and change however may not have fully taken into account three aspects of language planning, and particularly policy, which Cooper highlighted, and which I should like to explore further, basing comments in part on a recent study of language policy in Britain and France (Ager, 1996):

- 'to plan language is to plan society';
- 'language planning is "unlikely to succeed unless it is embraced and promoted by elites or counterelites"';
- 'language planning is typically motivated by efforts to secure or maintain interests, material or nonmaterial or both' (quotations from Cooper, 1989: 182–3).

The relationship between language planning and social planning is widely accepted, and indeed the coupling of multilingualism with multiculturalism proves the point. The language planning implemented by governments — their language policy — reflects their view of the society they would like to see. Britain's government and civil service in the late 1980s tried to impose a particular form of the standard language in education, as a direct result of a particular and very specific attempt to change society (Baker, 1993; Knight, 1990). French governments have long aimed at social cohesion and unity through an overt, monolingual language policy, reinforced in 1994. This rejects 'Anglo-Saxon' multiculturalism as divisive and offensive to French 'identity', which is based on the social contract the individual (not the group) makes with the state (Ager, 1996: 155–68). The two governments saw their language policy as both following and leading the social changes they hoped for. To their credit, Australia's governments in 1987 and 1991 openly declared their policies, too. But it should surprise no-one that the NPL is different from the ALLP. It took a long time to get language policy and multiculturalism taken seriously at policy level in Australia in the first place — Ozolins (1993: 206–20) dates the start of the serious attempt at the late 1970s, ten years or more before the NPL, and identifies the governmental interest as 'the solution of an appropriate political vehicle at a very critical period of government expenditure and suspicion of potentially expensive government programs'. It was convenient for government to appear to respond to a proposal which fitted (or was adapted to fit) its own political priorities at the time, and these changed between 1987 and 1991 as Thatcherism hit Australia. The same political purposes are very evident in tracking why literacy schemes in France and Britain were initiated in the way they were: the French did it in 1981–4 because they were stung into action by the European Parliament, and they associated illiteracy with poverty because they wanted to institute an anti-poverty, anti-deprivation scheme to show the differences between Mitterrand's Socialists and Giscard d'Estaing's Right-wingers. The British were determined to demonstrate that illiteracy was caused by the 'trendy sixties' policies of teacher training colleges, but the motive was equally ideological (Ager, 1996: 77–84). In both these cases the policies were either taken over, adapted or modified in order to fit political priorities, and it would be astounding if the Australian picture were different. As I understand it from talking to some of those involved, the NPL was accepted, perhaps less because it 'was based on a sophisticated rationale' as Michael Clyne notes, but because it responded to the two major political priorities of being seen to do something for the indigenous and immigrant groups who were clamouring for recognition and to demonstrate the economic necessity of capitalising on English (together with the shift towards foreign languages of economic importance). From a cynical point of view (and how can anybody not be cynical when confronted with the political world!), it was necessary for the activists to sell the policy idea to government by putting an economic spin on it, but unfortunately this was the only (or at least the main) angle the politicians were interested in. Selling the NPL on the basis of the good it would do Australia's economic future predestined the changes in the ALLP which took the economic argument further. Again, the British and the French can show similar examples of a takeover by politicians, in pursuance of their own ideology, of policy ideas or arguments made by activists. There are two examples here which show how quickly ideas were dropped when they didn't fit changed circumstances, or were poorly received. The French government seized on policy proposals which fitted its priorities in the anti-sexist language fiasco of the Roudy Commission in the late 1980s (Ager, 1996: 179–82). The howls of male laughter which met these meant the Government hid the proposals in a bland document issued the day they went out of power in 1986. Similarly, 1992 Charter initiatives in the UK under John Major have been swept out of the way, and the Plain English Campaign, which backed them and a number of other Tory initiatives on language, has been reduced to begging for a say in new Inland Revenue self-assessment documentation.

In this analysis Michael Clyne's choice of words ('economic rationalism' instead of 'neo-liberalism' or 'Thatcherism' for short) is absolutely right: neo-liberalism is rational because it follows the dictates of a particular ideology, and the language policy which follows is dictated by the same ideology of social engineering. The 'rationality' of the policies is founded on one ideology of social engineering: once the ideology changes, language policy necessarily, and rationally, follows. From this point of view, backlash to language policies is about the political acceptability of the social engineering policies involved. There is a good side to this bleak prospect, of course: in democracies, governments change and there is a policy swing. Just as neo-liberalism has been replaced by more centrist economic policies under Blair, political change in Australia will bring about changes in social engineering, and hence language, priorities.

The second point concerns the role of elites and counterelites in the successful implementation of policy. Interest and pressure groups have a significant role to play in developing a policy through its various stages and particularly in shaping and directing it before it is publicly promoted (Smith, 1993). Clyne mentions the public discussion before the NPL and its lack before the change to ALLP, and there is no doubt that the organisation of language professionals and their coming together with ethnic associations in AACLAME had a significant effect, particularly after 1987. In the French case, the policy community within which language matters (on French) are discussed is so institutionalised, and so prestigious, that the main pressure group has members from the civil service and the influential Paris intelligentsia, and the atmosphere in which matters pertaining to French are discussed is like a hothouse (Ager, 1996: 126–31). There is little doubt that this elite participation in the process lies behind much of the constant mention of language matters in Press and Parliament and fosters the French conception of identity no matter which party is in power. It also ensures that language maintenance programmes in France get little mention. Although some languages are supposedly taught for this purpose in French education, they, like regional languages, are mostly relegated to out-of-hours classes and are generally taken by those at the bottom of the social ladder in order to make up the appropriate number of passes in the public examinations.

From this point of view it is particularly interesting to note that the backlash to multingual/multicultural policies in Australia seems to come from 'a mining and pastoral electorate', and that Hanson represents a 'provincial Queensland town with a large working class vote'. It may be that their perception that they — never the elite, and solidly opposed to it — have been let down by the political elite protecting somebody else's interests. Perhaps the new Howard government was sharp enough to catch the mood, as Michael Clyne suggests. In this analysis, a Right-wing party allies itself with those who see the urban intellectual, the 'woolly-minded liberal', as the protector of only one sort of disadvantaged group: in this case the new immigrant and the indigenous peoples. Such reversals of the normal behaviour of political parties in their perceptions of the social status of particular groups are numerous. History is full of examples of Tory-voting working class dockers (in the 1960s in the UK), of the innate conservatism of rural

French voters, and part of the attraction of the *Front National* is precisely that it projects itself as a party of the mass. In Northern Ireland, both Protestants and Catholics feel themselves to be the underdog. What is fascinating is to understand what exactly such electors reject: is their attitude just envy and selfishness, is it fear of the unknown and different, or is it awareness of the passing of their own elite status? Certainly the close association of (low) social class and language maintenance in both France and Britain means that elites from the host community seem to provide little support for maintenance, and relevant communities do not seem to be supporting this particular aspect of language policy either.

The question of material and nonmaterial benefits arising from a policy, and to whom they are directed — *cui bono?* — is in Cooper's view fundamental. If advantages are not seen to accrue to significant parts of the policy environment as a result of the implementation of the policy, then a feedback mechanism will ensure either that the policy is abandoned or that it is changed so that benefits do arise. Benefits are not solely economic: to have one's human and social rights recognised is also, obviously, a benefit. But who benefits economically from NPL and ALLP, and who would benefit more from the changes? Tollefson (1991: 172–88), relying particularly on a study of labour in Sydney, concluded that, first in manufacturing and now in services, the Australian 'expansion requires large numbers of people without skills, without advanced education, and without the capacity for organised struggle', and concluded that 'a key criterion for determining which people will fill this position is lack of proficiency in English language'. His conclusion is that language rights in Australia — for maintenance as well as for English — 'depend on economic status and power' and that education could do little unless the group was powerful enough to demand rather than ask. This sort of call to the red revolution sounds a little dated nowadays, partly because most of us have been fed with a diet of the opposite view for 20 years; but economic rationalists as power brokers seem to have decided that multiculturalism and multilingualism held few benefits for themselves, and may have prevented them getting access to an adequately flexible labour force. Backlash here has come from the power brokers not from the powerless, and reminds one to some extent of the objections put forward by the Confederation of British Industry to the new Welsh Language Act of 1993 (Ager, 1996: 168–76). Some of these included 'there is concern that applicants might be appointed for their linguistic skills rather than their ability'; 'the creation of any kind of barrier between Wales and the rest of the United Kindom must be prevented'; 'the language of commerce world-wide is English'; 'no additional costs should be imposed on business'. In this case, opposition to Welsh was unsuccessful in preventing the Act being passed, but did change it quite significantly.

So if backlash has come about, it might have come from a different ideology of social change; from rejection from the bottom, or those who see themselves as powerless; and from rejection from the top, by those who aren't getting sufficient advantage from the resources involved. Michael Clyne's analysis of the Australian situation at least shows that backlash has not been too severe, and that although there has been a swing of the pendulum, it has not reversed all the advances that have been made.

References

Ager, D.E. (1996) *Language Policy in Britain and France. The Processes of Policy*. London: Cassell Academic.

Baker, K. (1993) *The Turbulent Years. My Life in Politics*. London: Faber.

Bréchon, P. (ed) (1994) *Le discours politique en France. Evolution des idees partisanes*. Notes et Etudes documentaires 4996. Paris: La Documentation Française.

Knight, C. (1990) *The Making of Tory Education Policy, 1950–1986*. London: Falmer Press.

Ozolins, U. (1993) *The Politics of Language in Australia*. Cambridge: Cambridge University Press.

Smith, M.J. (1993) *Pressure, Power and Policy: State Autonomy and Policy Networks in Britain and the United States*. Hemel Hempstead: Harvester Wheatsheaf.

Tollefson, J.W. (1991) *Planning Language, Planning Inequality*. London: Longman.

Language Maintenance or Language Fetishisation? A Response to Michael Clyne

Helen Kelly-Holmes
School of Languages and European Studies, Aston University, Aston Triangle,
Birmingham B4 7ET, UK

One of the most telling points made about the relationship between language and identity during the debate which followed Michael Clyne's seminar in Aston in May 1997 was not related to the use of a minority language but rather in relation to the use of English. Jenny Cheshire told how English is often preferred as a lingua franca among youth in multilingual Switzerland because they feel it is the language that best expresses their culture, a culture and identity which other young people not only in different linguistic regions in Switzerland, but elsewhere in Europe and the world also share. Does this mean that Switzerland's multilingualism has failed? Is this further evidence of English global hegemony? Or, is it instead simply that these young people have, through the sharing of a culture and a language, developed another identity which they choose to express in their own way, a choice that should be respected.

While I am sympathetic to the cause of language maintenance and in awe of the achievements of those who have campaigned for it and continue to do so in Australia and other countries, I do find many of the assumptions behind the unquestioned truth that languages should be maintained somewhat disturbing. It is not that I think languages should simply be allowed to die, but I do think we should always keep a critical eye on what is trying to be achieved, for whom and why. I do not work in the area of language maintenance and so my response here is based solely on my own personal experience as one of the objects of such policies and initiatives rather than the motivations of those working for language maintenance.

A multilingual, multicultural society should surely be something greater than and different to the simple sum of its number of languages and cultures; something hybridised and hyphenated, something with different layers and dimensions, composed of heterogeneous, 'multi' citizens, whose identity 'is increasingly experienced as an unstructured, and at times even optional, background choice' (James, 1996: 35). However, such a result seems to the protagonists of multilingualism a failure. The objective instead appears to be to preserve in stone the culture and the language of particular groups, guarding against shift, loss and other violent attacks. Michael Clyne's comments about the maintenance of Italian is very telling in this regard,

> the second generation use of Italian is probably overstated because it often covers an Italian ethnolect of Australian English where a limited number of Italian items are embedded into English as the matrix language.

Is it realistic or even fair to expect anything else of these individuals? How can their Italian be the same as that spoken in Italy or even by their immigrant parents — their whole linguistic, social, geographic, political, cultural, etc. context is not the same. They have made their own language, an expression of their own hybridised identity and yet they are branded failures, responsible for a 'wastage of language resources'.

Sir Ninian Stephen's observations are also evidence of this desire to confine individuals to an identity which they should continue simply because others have deemed that it should be continued. How can he expect children and grand-children of overseas-born Australians to 'retain' a culture that is not actually theirs? To expect this is to deny the validity of their own culture and identity.

To the outsider and often to the objects of language maintenance policies and initiatives, the motivations and attitudes of those promoting multilingualism and language maintenance must sometimes appear puzzling. Where the State attempts to impose a uniform language on its members either oblivious to, or in a direct attempt to undermine, the diversity of cultures, languages and traditions, its arrogance is rightly condemned. However, the same arrogance can be heard in many of the arguments raised by those campaigning for linguistic minority groups: the assumption of a homogeneous group, the disregard for those who live between groups, the demand for exclusive group loyalty, the attempt to impose an identity, and the equation of a chosen language of certain members of that group and with a unifying identity. Through such a process, the language itself becomes a fetish; its communicative or utility value becomes secondary to its symbolic value, it comes to have a meaning independent of its origins — it is no longer a means of communicating, but a badge of a stereotyped and limiting identity. Cultural and linguistic imperialism is not the preserve of colonising outsiders and global media.

Perhaps I should at this point explain my own background, since it inevitably provides the context for my comments in relation to Michael Clyne's paper and the debate and responses that follow it. The experience of being socialised into an ideal of a Gaelic Ireland through excessive and compulsory Irish language teaching — often at the expense of other subjects — has left me with an abhorrence of the over-ideologisation of language and the simplistic equation of language with identity. The failed experiment of language revival in post-independence Ireland has many causes, but the fact that Irish is not now the language of everyday life in Ireland is in no small way due to the fact that the language was hijacked by ideologues and imbued with values, qualities, histories far removed from the everyday culture lived by individuals. As Ó Laoire (1995) points out, the linguistic nationalism of the State espoused an

> image of the speaker in the Gaeltacht as a rural, Catholic, traditionalist peasant. In parts of the Republican movement, this model was advanced as the 'perfect Irishman'; this was the romantic philosophy of the Irish Ireland model. In reality, for the great mass of the population, this image was very complex. (p. 239)

Thus, embracing the language involved putting on an identity strait-jacket, which ordained that being 'Irish' was being Catholic, white, Celtic, nationalist (or even republican — it is not for nothing that the IRA's newspaper is called *'An Phoblacht'* rather than *'The Republic'* and the graffitied slogan of the IRA is *'Tiocfaidh ár lá'* not 'Our day will come') and, above all, not British — something which did nothing to help the Diaspora to come to terms with their own hyphenated identity or to ease tension and hostility in Northern Ireland, much of which is due to the insistence on group loyalty and the failure to acknowledge the possibility of multiple identities. Growing up in Ireland, the cultural imperialists lived in Dublin, not in London or Hollywood. This was not simply the feeling among many of my peers learning Irish as a second language at school; the resentment was at times perhaps stronger in the Irish speaking Gaeltacht:

> The failure to reconcile romantic nationalism and nationalist myth with the realities of Gaeltacht life has been a conspicuous element in the failure to save the language ... there is little common ground between Gaeltacht workers who see language as a tool, to be discarded for a better one when it becomes obsolete and nationalists who believe Irish people should speak Irish because they are Irish and regardless of utilitarian considerations. (Hindley, 1990: 212)

For many young people learning the language, the inevitable outcome — like the second generation Italian speakers — was failure, success in the language being seen as the preserve of the *'Gaeilgeoirí'*,

> a sort of Masonic Order of initiates who use language qualifications to exclude others from the competition for jobs.[1] The elitism and 'more patriotic than thou' attitudes do not help the living language at all and to ordinary people make Irish seem something to 'put them down'. (Hindley, 1990: 176)

It is only in recent years that the error of such cultural nationalist policies has been identified. The tokenism of the majority's relationship with the language (cf. Edwards, 1985) has been acknowledged and rather than being presented as a failure of revivalism, it is seen as acceptable and even positive (cf. Ó Laoire, 1995) that most people in Ireland have some knowledge of and relationship with the language. Parallel with and inherently linked to this acknowledgement has come the realisation that identity and culture in Ireland has been positively enhanced by engaging with the global and recognising the hyphenated existence which many individuals lead and which defies identity categorisation. Rather than threatening Irish identity, these realisations have, if anything, served to strengthen a sense of non-chauvinistic pride in a new hybridised version (cf. for instance O'Toole, 1997).

The effect of all this on the relationship with the Irish language has been interesting, exemplified by the new Irish-medium television channel *Teilifís na Gaelige (TnaG)*, which is attracting positive viewing figures.[2] Rather than being conceived on the basis of an overtly cultural-nationalist model that would impart the prescribed identity through appropriate programmes, the station's main objective is instead entertainment. Its diet thus consists of quiz shows, pop music videos (rather than exclusively Irish traditional music), current affairs programmes, dubbed programmes etc. Rather than the uncompromising purism of the past, the station instead provides English sub-titles and uses English in certain programmes. And people watch it. Of course, some of these already have fluent Irish which they wish to maintain and others have a strong sense of identity and watch it for ideological reasons, but many are simply curious — they want to try out their Irish, to see how much they understand. This is possible, because nobody is telling them to watch the channel or defining for them what watching it means to their identity and the programmes themselves do not conform to a strict definition of 'Irishness'. And, no doubt, their Irish improves because they do so, as a side-product of amusement. The channel is simply one among a plethora of national and international offerings available in today's Ireland, all contributing to the identities of individuals and groups.

The case of Ireland is of course different to the situation of minority language groups in Australia, Britain and elsewhere. However, this does not mean that there are not lessons that can be learned about the fetishisation and ideologisation of a language. The Irish example reminds us that the relationship between language and identity is far more complex than it is sometimes assumed in the quest for language maintenance as a means of group identity maintenance. Identity is a by-product of language and a common language is in turn the product of a shared identity; the process is interrelated, the result of sharing a common context within which that language is spoken and from which that language originates. When we make identity the sole aim and language the means, when we make the relationship explicit and simplistic, the process is bound to fail, except where individuals feel an identity strongly to the exclusion of others and wish to use their language to underline this fact.

While understanding the fears of those trying to keep language communities in existence, a defensive and reactionary approach is, perhaps, not the best way. Even the term 'language maintenance' conjures up the image of a monolithic construction. The objective of those maintaining it is, above all, to prevent its demolition, so they carry out the necessary repair work to keep it from falling down completely. The building itself becomes the end rather than what people do within it or what it is used for. Even if nobody visits it or works in it, at least it is still standing. It is almost too clichéd to say that language is not an institution, it is not a static thing, it is something that is lived, but when using the term 'language maintenance' perhaps we need to remind ourselves of this.

Unless the language enables individuals to live their culture, rather than it simply being presented to them as a fetished icon of a prescribed culture to which they should subscribe, unless they are allowed to work out their own relationship with the language and the culture, instead of being drafted in as foot-soldiers in the defence of that language and culture, and unless their membership of other groups is not seen as a threat, then the language is already lost. It is brave and admirable to battle against a dominating culture and language, but it is braver still to say to new generations, do what you will with this language, make it your own. The consequence of such an attitude is change, rather than loss.

Notes

1. Certified competence in Irish being a necessary qualification for a number of positions in the civil and public service and in the education system.
2. *Sunday Tribune*, 7 September 1997.

References

Edwards, J. (1985) *Language, Society and Identity*. Oxford: Blackwell in association with André Deutsch.
Hindley, R. (1990) *The Death of the Irish Language: A Qualified Obituary*. London: Routledge.
James, P. (1996) *Nation Formation: Towards a Theory of Abstract Community*. London: Sage.
Ó Laoire, M. (1995) An historical perspective on the revival of Irish outside the Gaeltacht, 1880–1930 with reference to the revitalization of Hebrew. In S. Wright (ed.) *Language and the State: Revitalization in Israel and Éire*. Clevedon: Multilingual Matters.
O'Toole, F. (1997) *The Ex-Isle of Erin — Images of a Global Ireland*. Dublin: New Ireland Books.

Michael Clyne comments:

I fear I may have made myself open to misinterpretation. Firstly, let me defend Sir Ninian Stephen. What I think he is saying is that bilingualism is worthwhile and, far from being un-Australian, can be a national asset. He is not branding children of migrants as failures but distancing himself from the old position of the British ascendancy that speaking another language in addition to English is something that you should be ashamed of. There is, in my opinion, no assumption that you have to speak the language in a particular way. Language maintenance in my statistics is defined as speaking a language other than English in the home. There is no question that people should be forced to maintain a language but they should receive encouragement and support because this provides for a more cohesive and more harmonious Australia, where people feel that they fit in, a more interesting one, and one that strengthens links with the cultures represented and the countries concerned (perhaps this is part of my answer to Stephen May). The situation is quite different from that in Ireland. In Australia an open national ideology has developed in which 'exclusive group loyalty' is not popular in any groups of the population.

On purism, I must say that most of the studies of language contact in Australia have been descriptive rather than prescriptive. There should be a possibility for people to develop (and become literate in) a variety of the language in which they can communicate with the countries in which the language has national status. But this should in no way detract from the varieties that are employed in communities and families in Australia and which are appropriate to the needs of the speakers in the Australian context.